C000050982

At Hame Wi' Freedom

Other books edited by Eberhard Bort published
in collaboration with the Carrying Stream Festival

BORNE ON THE CARRYING STREAM:
The Legacy of Hamish Henderson
ISBN: 978-1-907676-01-7 (PBK)
ISBN: 978-1-907676-16-1 (e-book)

'TIS SIXTY YEARS SINCE:
The 1951 Edinburgh People's Festival Ceilidh
and the Scottish Folk Revival
ISBN: 978-1-907676-10-9 (PBK)
ISBN: 978-1-907676-11-6 (e-book)

At Hame Wi' Freedom

Essays on Hamish Henderson and the Scottish Folk Revival

Editor
Eberhard Bort
University of Edinburgh

Copyright © Contributors, 2012

AT HAME WI' FREEDOM
ESSAYS ON HAMISH HENDERSON
AND THE SCOTTISH FOLK REVIVAL
EDITED BY EBERHARD BORT

First published 2012 by Grace Note Publications
in collaboration with the Carrying Stream Festival
Grange of Locherlour, Ochtertyre, PH7 4JS, Scotland

www.gracenotepublications.co.uk
books@gracenotereading.co.uk

ISBN: 978-1-907676-17-8 (PBK)
ISBN: 978-1-907676-18-5 (e-book)

All rights reserved

A catalogue record for this book is available from the British Library

Front cover: Summer 1944 – the victorious partisans: Hamish Henderson (left) with Luigi Castiglione and his driver Ivan in the famous 'Bandiera Rossa' (red banner) jeep. Courtesy of Felicity Henderson.

For two Margarets

————

Margaret MacPherson and Margaret Bennett

————

and

Kätzel Henderson

Acknowledgements

This book is published on the occasion of the eleventh Carrying Stream Festival, ten years after the death of Hamish Henderson (1919-2002), Scotland's foremost folklorist, poet, songwriter and political activist. Thanks are due to his widow, Kätzel Henderson, for her continuing patronage. The Festival is organised by Edinburgh Folk Club – a big thanks to my fellow committee members Kathleen Smith, John Jessiman, Allan McMillan and Anne Hand – and to Jack Foster, our soundman.

This volume would not have been possible without the contributors working to rather tight schedules. Thanks for coming up with the goods! Pino Mereu deserves a special mention for allowing us to publish his Anzio sequence with the accompanying Scots translation by Tom Hubbard. *Anzio Pipe Band* was originally published as *Bonsai 8* by Edizioni Empirìa in February 2012. We are grateful to the editor Marisa Di Iorio for the permission to republish the poems. Margaret MacPherson helped with the translation from the Italian. Pino would like to add that the Anzio Pipe Band was made up of pipers from the Gordon Highlanders, the Seaforth Highlanders and the Royal Scots Fusiliers. He also did some research on the tunes they played: among them were 'Fareweel to the Creeks', 'Tulloch Gorum', 'The Desperate Battle', 'The Siege of Delhi', 'Mount Etna', 'The Roads to Rome', 'Ballad of Anzio' and 'The Gallant Forty Twa'. The accompanying photos are reproduced courtesy of Kätzel Henderson. Pino would like to thank Hamish Henderson, his fellow poet, singer and Scottish friend, for his lyrics, his stories and his life were a fount of inspiration for his Anzio poems. Hamish was a combatant at Anzio as a Captain in the ranks of the Highland Division and formed the Anzio Pipe Band. He would also like to express his thanks to Roger Waters for his lyrics on *The Final Cut* by Pink Floyd. Roger Waters lost his father, Eric Fletcher Waters, at Anzio in February 1944. Pino is also grateful to Kätzel Henderson for her generous and kind support; and to Timothy Neat, for having kindly provided the photographs contained herein, delivered to him many years ago by Hamish, and for his constant and loving suggestions. And a final thanks to

Michelle Müller for pushing Pino to revisit the Anzio Pipe Band.

An earlier version of George Gunn's chapter appeared in Kenneth Roy's *Scottish Review* and is here included with kind permission; Belle Stewart's 'The Berryfields o Blair' is reproduced with the kind permission of Sheila Stewart.

The photograph on the cover – the victorious partisans: Hamish Henderson (left) with Luigi Castiglione and his driver Ivan in the famous 'Bandiera Rossa' (red banner) jeep, summer 1944. Courtesy of Felicity Henderson. The image of the Hamish Henderson bust in the Blairgowrie library, below, was taken by Maurice Fleming who also provided the historical images of Blairgowrie for his chapter. The photos illustrating Alison McMorland's chapter come from Elizabeth Stewart's family album, the one with Alison and Elizabeth Stewart singing together was taken by Geordie McIntyre. Allan McMillan, photo-chronicler of Edinburgh Folk Club (see www.efcphotos.co.uk), has kindly supplied a photo gallery of last year's Carrying Stream Festival and of Owen Dudley Edwards' Hamish Henderson Lecture. The Annual Hamish Henderson Lecture at the Carrying Stream Festival is organised in partnership between Edinburgh Folk Club and the Edinburgh City Council – our thanks go in particular to Councillor Deidre Brock and to Jo Navarro.

Last, but certainly not least, huge thanks go to Gonzalo Mazzei of Grace Note Publications for his boundless patience and his immeasurable input to this volume.

Bust of Hamish Henderson by
Andrew Morrow in Blairgowrie Library.

Contents

Photos and Illustrations

---

[1] RCS = Royal Conservatoire of Scotland (the former RSAMD).

Introduction

Eberhard Bort

This publication marks the tenth anniversary of Hamish Henderson's death in 2002. It is the third book of a loose trilogy which began with *Borne on the Carrying Stream* (Grace Note, 2010), followed by *'Tis Sixty Years Since* (Grace Note, 2011) – all revolving around the life and legacy of Hamish Henderson and the Scottish Folk Revival he did so much to inspire and sustain.

At Hame wi' Freedom focuses on Hamish Henderson's involvement in the revival, his association with Perthshire and the North-East, and the emergence of his poetic voice. But at the core of this volume are two pieces inspired by Hamish Henderson: Pino Mereu's poetic evocation of the Anzio (Beachhead) Pipe Band and Owen Dudley Edwards' Hamish Henderson Memorial Lecture of 2011.

Borne on the Carrying Stream was built around a handful of the Hamish Henderson Memorial Lectures given annually at Edinburgh Folk Club's Carrying Stream Festival and tried to assess the legacy of the great folklorist, poet, songwriter and political activist for the twenty-first century; the second book had as its focus the sixtieth anniversaries of both the first Edinburgh People's Festival Ceilidh, organised and compered by Hamish, and the foundation of the School of Scottish Studies at Edinburgh University in 1951 – Hamish's academic home for the rest of his life. It gave Hamish's own account of the Festival Ceilidhs as well as Ewan McVicar's research into the recordings Alan Lomax made of the 1951 – released in 2006 as an album by Rounder Records (Rounder CD 1786).

The People's Festival Ceilidhs were a major catalyst for the burgeoning Folk Revival in Scotland. The anniversary celebrations in 2011 were, to say the least, a memorable occasion (see the photographs of Allan McMillan at the end of this introduction to get an impression). Back at Oddfellows' Hall, the original venue of the 1951 shindig, now Malone's Irish bar, a fine crowd gathered on 9 November 2011 to join with a host of musicians in the celebrations, and at the Pleasance Theatre a veritable who's who of Scotland's traditional music scene, all connected with the School of Scottish Studies and the Royal Conservatoire, gave a breath-taking performance of over three hours. Phil Cunningham provided, in his inimitably genial way, musical guidance for both evenings; Ewan McVicar and Adam McNaughtan excelled as witty and knowledgeable comperes for the two anniversary nights. In the footsteps of John Burgess, piper Donald Mackay opened proceedings with a birl on the Highland Pipes.

These were events that knew no generational or linguistic barriers. There were tradition bearers in Scots and Gaelic like Sheila Stewart, Jock Duncan, Margaret Bennett, Rod Paterson, Gordeanna McCulloch, Talitha MacKenzie, Margaret Callan and Jean Redpath, younger singers like Lucy Pringle, Chris Wright, Steve Byrne and Scott Gardiner, musicians like Patsy Seddon, Gary West, Josh Dickson and Barnaby Brown – and Phil Cunningham brought along a hugely talented bunch of musicians and singers from the Royal Conservatoire in Glasgow to round things off with a flourish.

A particularly thrilling pleasure was the presence of Flora MacNeil at Oddfellows' Hall, where she famously sang in the 1951 Ceilidh. Sharing the stage, sixty years on, with her daughter Maggie MacInnes, was a highlight of the celebrations. Hayden Murphy's remarks about the two, penned on the occasion of their 1984 Edinburgh Folk Festival appearance, could easily have been written about this performance:

> They sang and played beautifully. As Flora MacNeil commented: "When people did not have instruments they sang – forth." Her daughter played the harp and the music fused in duet by these two is both a treat and a formidable weapon. It was lovely.[1]

Edinburgh Folk Club on its own could not have managed to organise these events – they were very much the collaborative result of EFC and the School of Scottish Studies – in particular Cathlin Macauley and Gary West – and the Royal Conservatoire – first and foremost Talitha MacKenzie and Phil Cunningham. It was very nice that the

---

[1] Hayden Murphy, 'Edinburgh Folk Festival', *The Glasgow Herald*, 9 April 1984.

anniversary celebrations were noted in the Scottish Parliament, thanks to Rob Gibson MSP, who lodged a Motion on Hamish's birthday which received cross-party support:

Motion S4M-01322: Rob Gibson, Caithness, Sutherland and Ross, Scottish National Party, Date Lodged: 11/11/2011

The Parliament applauds the 10th Carrying Stream Festival, held in Edinburgh from 9 to 16 November 2011; notes that the festival was formed to celebrate the life and legacy of Hamish Henderson, the renowned folklorist who died in 2002; especially praises what it considers the organisers' outstanding success in mounting a 60th anniversary concert in the original venue that saw the first People's Festival Ceilidh in 1951, which presented traditional Gaelic and Scots singing and piping to an enthralled urban audience; welcomes that, 60 years on, on 10 November 2011 the knowledgable audience was treated to what it considers unforgettable performances from a few surviving singers; notes that the festival also displayed today's crop of young singers and players, many of whom are studying for degrees in traditional music at the Conservatoire in Glasgow, which it considers a modern symbol of the popularity and strength of traditional music in Scottish culture today, and considers that Scottish roots music, first brought to urban audiences by Hamish Henderson in the People's Festival Ceilidh in 1951, today fills the largest halls in the land.

Supported by: Margaret Burgess, John Finnie, Bill Kidd, Richard Lyle, Joan McAlpine, Kenneth Gibson, Angus MacDonald, Kevin Stewart, Linda Fabiani, Jim Eadie, Mike MacKenzie, Mary Scanlon, Maureen Watt, Patricia Ferguson, David Torrance, Humza Yousaf, Jean Urquhart, Nigel Don, James Dornan, Annabelle Ewing, Jamie Hepburn, Colin Beattie, Stuart McMillan, Gil Paterson, Stewart Maxwell.[2]

---

[2] <http://www.scottish.parliament.uk/parliamentarybusiness/28877.aspx?SearchType=Simple&Keyword=carrying%20Stream&ExactPhrase=True&DateChoice=4&MSPId=2675&SortBy=DateSubmitted&ResultsPerPage=10>

Last year's Hamish Henderson Lecture was delivered, in his trademark bravura style, by Edinburgh's most famous living Irishman, Owen Dudley Edwards, musically supported by his wife Bonnie. It attracted a packed and spellbound audience at the City Chambers. As published in this volume, it does not only record Owen's longstanding acquaintance with Hamish Henderson – he knew him so well, he says, that they were not on speaking terms for sixteen years – but, more importantly, the role Hamish played in the publication of *The Red Paper on Scotland*[3] and *The People's Past*[4] – and particularly in introducing Gordon Brown to the thinking of Antonio Gramsci and persuading at least parts of the Labour party that small 'n' nationalism is compatible with democratic socialism and a distinctly international outlook.

Having thus paid homage to Hamish, Owen embarks on a trenchant discussion of the history and nature of sectarian singing. This, too, is relevant in any discussion of Hamish Henderson – he had a healthy aversion to any form of bigotry and sectarianism, as can be seen in his letters protesting against triumphalist Orange marches and those exposing Catholic nationalist bigotry.[5] His work in Belfast in the late 1940s had been most instructive.

The final chapter attempts to follow up on Hamish's political activities, his interventions and the evolution of his political outlook, from his pre-War Cambridge communism to the nationalism of the National Covenant, the CND marches and anti-apartheid campaign, his involvement in the short-lived Scottish Labour Party, his turning down that OBE from the Thatcher government, the anti-Poll Tax protests, and his unwavering commitment to Home Rule for Scotland.

At the Carrying Stream Festival in 2008, Pino Mereu, the organiser of the Hamish Henderson Folk Club in Rome, gave a moving Lecture on Hamish among the Italian partisans. Earlier this year, he published a sequence of poems on the Anzio Pipe Band. His twin inspirations were Hamish's *Elegies for the Dead in Cyrenaica* (1948) and *The Final Cut* (1983) by Pink Floyd. Like Pino,

---

[3] Gordon Brown (ed.), *The Red Paper on Scotland*, Edinburgh: EUSPB, 1975.

[4] Edward J. Cowan (ed.), *The People's Past: Scottish Folk – Scottish History*, Edinburgh: EUSPB/Polygon, 1980.

[5] See, for example, the letters on pp.52 and 216 in Hamish Henderson, *The Armstrong Nose: Selected Letters*, edited by Alec Finlay, Edinburgh: Polygon, 1996.

Roger Waters (who wrote all the songs for *The Final* Cut) lost his father at the six-month battle of Anzio. To lift morale in what had become a "killing zone,"[6] Hamish did not only write songs for the English and Scottish battalions under siege, he also formed what became known as the Beachhead Pipe Band, touring the Anzio battlefield and visiting field hospitals. The Pipe Band took part in the Allied advance on Rome, playing its part in the celebrations:

> Hamish informed the Scottish brigade commanders that the entry into Rome must not be a purely American triumph. He insisted that the Beachhead Pipe Band should play a major role in the celebrations and that it could put an indelibly Scottish signature on the Liberation – like nothing else.[7]

Or, as Hamish expressed it in 'The Roads to Rome':

> But noo ye'll hear the pipers play
> Afore St Peter's Dome
> And Scotland tells the world today
> That oor road led to Rome.[8]

The reception by the Italians was enthusiastic and, on Hamish's suggestion, a radio broadcast was made and 'via Movietone News ... the sound of the Pipe Band – conceived in blood on the Anzio Beachhead – went round the world.'[9]

Pino's poems are intensely evocative of the Anzio experience; they are personal reflections on the battle, the fallen and the survivors, about loss, memory and history, and they take us right into the battle zone and the carnage of Anzio itself. We invited the renowned Scots poet and translator Tom Hubbard to 'transcreate' the poems into Scots and, together with a slightly more prosaic English translation (for those of us with neither Italian nor Scots), we present them at the heart of this volume.

---

[6] Timothy Neat, *Hamish Henderson: A Biography, Vol.I: The Making of the Poet, 1919-1953*, Edinburgh: Birlinn, 2007, p.129.

[7] *Ibid.*, p.137.

[8] Hamish Henderson, Collected Poems and Songs, edited by Raymond Ross, Edinburgh: Curly Snake, 2000, p.96

[9] Timothy Neat, *Hamish* Henderson, Vol.I, p.139.

Maurice Fleming who, urged on by Hamish Henderson, had in the 1950s become a 'scout' for the School of Scottish Studies, tracking down singers and storytellers in Perthshire, particularly among the Travellers in berryfields of Blair, shares some choice reminiscences with us of the early and formative years of Hamish in Blairgowrie. We follow that chapter with the famous song Maurice 'discovered' for Hamish, Belle Stewart's 'The Berryfields o Blair'.

In the 1960s, Hamish had a triumphant return to Blairgowrie, when the newly-formed Traditional Music and Song Association of Scotland (TMSA) organised the pioneering Blairgowrie Folk Festivals. Jim Bainbridge, melodeon player extraordinaire, was there, and – although those were the 1960s – he does remember the second and third of the festivals which he attended and played at.

Ewan McVivar gives us a glimpse at the Scottish Folk Revival at work, in the correspondence between Hamish and Arthur Argo who, fifty years ago, founded the Aberdeen Folk Club. Arthur Argo (1935-1981) was the great-grandson of folk collector Gavin Greig and a tireless promoter of the folk revival, collecting and recording with Hamish Henderson in the north-east, working for the BBC as radio producer, and publishing *Chapbook*, the leading magazine of the Revival.

Alison McMorland provides some background to her labour of love, editing the life-story of Elizabeth Stewart of the Fetterangus Stewarts. Again, Hamish Henderson's encouragement is duly noted, but also his respect for the travelling people and their vital contribution to keep traditional Scottish oral culture alive – as is evident in Elizabeth Stewart's remarkable repertoire of songs and stories.

Fred Freeman gave the very first Hamish Henderson Memorial Lecture at the inaugural Carrying Stream Festival in November 2002. Here, he discussed the emergence of Hamish's poetic and song-writing voice, focusing on his 'unhomogeneous' use of languages and registers. George Gunn uses Hamish as his reference point for a meditation on the positioning of poetry and the poet in contemporary society. Hayden Murphy, himself a noted Irish poet and, between 1967 and 1978, the editor, publisher and distributor of *Broadsheet*, recalls his association with Hamish as a fellow Festival goer, and also how some of his poems found their way into *Broadsheet*.

Since his death in 2002, Hamish Henderson has been honoured in many ways: festivals, memorials, Tim Neat's two-volume biography, books, lectures and awards in his name. The Scottish Parliament had a debate on 27 March 2002, based on a Motion by Cathie Peattie MSP, where MSPs across the parties paid their respects.

When the parliament opened, a quotation from 'The Freedom Come-All-Ye' was chiselled into a slab of Corennie Granite from Aberdeenshire on the Canongate Wall:

> So, cam' all ye at hame wi' freedom
> Never heed whit the hoodies croak for doom
> In your hoose a' the bairns o' Adam
> Can find breid, barley bree an' painted room.[10]

He would have liked that. And maybe the Parliament finds a way of commemorating him inside the building as well in future times? But the best way of commemorating him is to engage with his work. The future of Hamish's letters and papers is key to that.

The signs are very promising that, ten years after Hamish Henderson's death, the negotiations about his archive are nearing a satisfactory conclusion. Having that archive in the public domain, eventually, properly curated and made available for research purposes will open a new chapter for Scottish folklore studies and help to secure Hamish Henderson's legacy for future generations. Steve Byrne and Chris Wright of the Hamish Henderson Trust[11] are to be congratulated for cataloguing and temporarily archiving the collection from July 2011 to March 2012.[12] Making Hamish's papers and letters – more than 10,000 of them – more widely accessible while many of his friends and colleagues are still active in public life – people ideally placed to conduct research and promote his legacy – will undoubtedly help to keep the life and work of Hamish Henderson in the public consciousness now and in the future.

---

[10] Hamish Henderson, *Collected Poems and Songs*, p.143.

[11] www.hendersontrust.org.

[12] See Steve Byrne, 'Working on the Hamish Henderson Papers', in E Bort (ed.) *'Tis Sixty Years Since: The 1951 Edinburgh People's Festival Ceilidh and the Scottish Folk Revival*, Ochtertyre: Grace Note Publications, 2011, pp.172-186

The trust plans to complement the inventory of Hamish's correspondence with a similar catalogue of his manuscript items, which include poems and songs as yet unpublished. Then there are his many notebooks and diaries, which contain an array of information on all aspects of his career. The thousands of other items, including newspaper clippings and articles, photographs and other papers must also be properly recorded and detailed.[13]

There is plenty of work waiting for curators and researchers interested in Hamish Henderson's life and legacy.

The then Education and Culture Deputy Minister, Elaine Murray MSP, closed the Parliament's debate in 2002 with the following words:

Hamish Henderson supported many causes, including nuclear disarmament, the anti-apartheid movement, international socialism, home rule and, possibly, independence for Scotland.

Hamish Henderson's work will help us to appreciate the value of our living tradition. To appreciate and value our Scottish culture and traditional arts would perhaps be the greatest memorial to Hamish Henderson that we could create. In celebrating our culture and in celebrating Scotland, we celebrate him; in celebrating him, we celebrate our culture.[14]

If this book can play its humble part in doing just that, it has served its purpose. I am again deeply grateful to Gonzalo Mazzei of Grace Note Publications for is immeasurable input and enthusiasm. I can only hope it gives him as much pleasure as me that these books on Hamish Henderson and the Scottish Folk Revival are published in Perthshire, the place that, as Maurice Fleming reminds us, made the man.

---

[13] Chris Wright, 'A man of passion and principle', *The Scots Magazine*, August 2012, pp.51-53; p.53.

[14] Elaine Murray, Scottish Parliament debate, 27 March 2002, <http://archive.scottish.parliament.uk/business/businessBulletin/bb-02/bb-03-12f.htm>.

© Allan McMillan

Oddfellows Hall – Forrest Rd, Edinburgh, 9 Nov. 2011

Steve Byrne, Lucy Pringle & Chris Wright

© Allan McMillan

© Allan McMillan

Ewan McVicar

Maggie MacInnes

©Allan McMillan

©Allan McMillan

Flora MacNeil

Sheila Stewart

© Allan McMillan

©Allan McMillan

Jock Duncan

Margaret Bennett and Nathan Salsburg
at the 'Alan Lomax in Scotland' Workshop

© Allan McMillan

© Allan McMillan

Scott Gardiner

Ewan, Phil Cunningham and students from the Royal Conservatoire of Scotland

© Allan McMillan

© Allan McMillan

Phil Cunningham and students from
the Royal Conservatoire of Scotland

Hamish Henderson: The Early Years

Maurice Fleming[1]

Hamish Henderson was such a familiar and kenspeckle figure in the streets and howffs of Edinburgh over so many years you could be forgiven for thinking that he had always lived there. But Hamish was a Perthshire man, and the scenes and people he knew in his earliest years made a lasting impression on him and were a huge influence on his character and career.

He was born in a villa on the outskirts of Blairgowrie, East Perthshire on 11 November 1919. The house, Ramleh, is just minutes along the road from where I am writing this, and I pass it every day. Ramleh is a handsome house with a front garden. At the back it overlooks fields, the nearest planted this year (2012) with potatoes, but at that time, when owned by he Morrison family, it would amost certainly have been under raspberries, some of the famous 'Berryfields o' Blair' of Belle Stewart's famous song.

The house belonged to his grandparents, retired business people from Dundee, and their daughter, Janet Henderson, had come there to have her child. She had returned from nursing service in France and registered the birth of James Scott Henderson.

A few weeks later she took him to live in a rented cottage at the Spittal of Glenshee, sixteen miles north of Blairgowrie. The Spittal lies at the head of this lovely glen, and there has been a settlement here for centuries, an ideal spot for travellers to stop for rest and refreshment on their way to or from Braemar and Deeside. A little further north, the once notorious Devil's Elbow has been straightened out, but he young Hamish would hear stories of the hairpin bend and the accidents it caused.

More to the point, he heard local storytellers relate how the hero Diarmid, lover of Grainne, hunted down and slew a savage boar on Ben Gulabin, the hill above the cottage in which he and his mother were living. And then how Diarmid was cruelly tricked and died and lies buried with Grainne in a nearby grave.

---

[1] Born on the same road as Hamish Henderson, Maurice Fleming is uniquely placed to trace Hamish's childhood background.

When I recorded the tale from a local woman in the 1960s; Hamish told me he first climbed Gulabin with his mother at the age of four and searched, as I had done, for the Boar's Bed and other natural features associated with the Fingalian tale. It must have been one of the very first legends he heard, tough of course Glenshee then was full of them every step of the way, handed down in the old glen families. Not for nothing it is named Glenshee – the Glen of the Fairies.

During these formative years that he lived there he heard Gaelic spoken all around him – the old Perthshire Gaelic now, alas, extinct. Janet Henderson picked up some of it and took an interest in the Gaelic placenames up and down the glen. And of course there was singing and music. It was here he learned the lively 'Tail Toddle' which he sang on countless occasions. He learned to dance, too, having taken early lessons from a well known itinerant teacher, 'Dancie' Reid.

All in all, by the time he and Janet left the Spittal, Hamish had acquired from the robust glenners a grounding in Gaelic culture and a sympathy with rural attitudes which were to serve him well in later years when songhunting amongst country folk throughout Scotland.

But it was back to Ramleh Janet took him so that, at five, he could begin formal education at the school in Blairgowrie. There he was fortunate in his first teacher, Janet Peterkin, a lady from Moray who had a keen interest in Scottish songs and traditions. She quickly realised that here was a boy after her own heart. She would no doubt be aware, too, that he was fatherless.

A few years after Hamish, I was a pupil of Miss Peterkin, and I remember a gentle but firm teacher who presided over us like a kindly and protective mother hen. At this crucial stage in Hamish's development, her encouragement meant a great deal to him. He kept in touch with her, and when she retired he visited her in Lossiemouth. She, on her part, followed his career with close interest.

Janet Henderson and her son moved from Ramleh to another address in Blairgowrie, indeed thet moved three or four times. The late Adam Malcolm was a Blairgowrie man who became headmaster of the school in Alyth before retiring to his hometown. He told me how he first encountered Hamish when playing with pals in the street. "This strange boy came out of a doorway and asked if he could join in. I remember it clearly because he was wearing a kilt, very unusual in Blair. He and I got on well."

After schooldays, when Adam was at Edinburgh University, he met up with Hamish again. Adam was a bit of a stormy petrel, strongly in favour of Scottish independence and constantly at war with local authorities over issues concerning Blairgowrie. A doughty fighter on behalf of local causes, he and Hamish wold have a lot in common.

After the years spent in the remote glen cottage, it was a big change for Hamish to be living in a town where, at first, he knew no one. He adapted well. The fact he approached Adam Malcolm and his pals and asked to join them shows self-confidence and assurance. He might have felt swamped in the school by the sheer numbers of other children after the handful he had known at the Spittal but he quickly made friends among them and distinguished himself by vigorously defending a boy who was being bullied. This boy, Neil Grant, became a close friend.

But if the new location was rewarding foir him, it was less so for his mother. She was, by all accounts, a lively, intelligent, talented young woman with many interests – singing, music and languages among them. There must have been frustration and, in view of her unmarried state, real insecurity.

Her Perth Road neighbours told my mother she was "not much of a housewife." One of them reported seeing her empty the teapot out of the kitchen window! Each of the house-moves she made with Hamish in Blairgowrie was to a poorer quality home. This suggests money problems.

In the end she came to a momentous decision. They would leave Scotland. Hamish was to go to a boarding school in Devon, and she was to take a job as a housekeeper (ironic in view of what her neighbours said).

For both of them, it was good-bye to Perthshire.

Why did she take such a drastic step?

Janet Henderson had reached crisis point. There were several factors at play here. Shortage of money was almost certainly one. In spite of this she would be determined that her promising son receive the best education possible. It may be, too, that show was aware already of the cancer that was to cut short her life. This clever, vivacious young woman was to die in 1933.

When, in 1954, I told my mother that on a weekend visit to Edinburgh I had met a man called Hamish Henderson who had lived for a time along the road from us in Blairgowrie, she at once said: "I remember him – a little boy in a kilt." That kilt always marked him out (I had been too young to have any recollection of him or his mother).

He had fired me with enthusiasm for collecting. With a portable tape recorder Hamish lent me from the School of Scottish Studies I went in search of singers, and as it was Berrytime the campsites were full of travellers. Within a few days I was overwhelmed by the wealth of the material. So many singers, so many songs. I sent Hamish an urgent message urging him to come and join me. I added that I had found the woman who wrote 'The Berryfields o' Blair'. Hamish had collected a version and asked me to try to find it on its homeground. Now, here was its creator, Belle Stewart.

For Hamish it was a triumphant return to Blairgowrie. When he had left it for England all these years before, he could never have dreamed of such a homecoming. His collecting work in the berryfields that summer and succeeding ones is a major chapter in the history of Scottish folk song. For a time, Blairgowrie was the unofficial capital of folk song, the clear favourite for the first Traditional Music and Song Association (TMSA) Festival which was notable for the clutch of great traditional singers who appeared on the bill, many of them Hamish's discoveries.

After the manner of his leaving Blairgowrie it would not have been surprising if there had been some lingering bitterness. If there was, it must surely have been expunged by the welcome he received there and the role he saw it play in the Folk Revival. In the 1960s and '70s, I found him always delighted to make a return visit – and he still did so long after his collecting days were over. Of the Stewart family, Alex, Belle and Cathie were gone, but Sheila was still there and still singing. It was now she who sang 'The Berryfields o' Blair'.

And the town did hold happy memories for him. Take this verse:

> I climb with Neil the whinny Braes of Lornty.
>   Or walk my lane by drumly Ericht side.
> Under Glasclune we play the death of Comyn,
>   And fear, wee boys, the Auld Kirk's sin of pride.[2]

---

[2] Hamish Henderson, 'Ballad of the Twelve Stations of My Youth', Collected Poems and Songs, edited by Raymond Ross, Edinburgh: Curly Snake, 2000, p.23.

Neil was Neil Grant, his school friend. The Lornty is a lovely stream running through a hidden valley behind the town. Glasclune is a ruined castle few ever see as it can only be approached by foot. Perched on the edge of a steep ravine, it would be an exciting place for any adventurous laddie.

The casle is the subject of another poem, 'Glasclune and Drumlochy' – it tells of the feud between the Blairs of Glasclune and their near neighbours, the Herons of Drumlochy. The Blairs brought the feud to an end when they obtained a 'secret weapon', a cannon, and smashed Drumlochy's walls:

> Drumlochy focht fair,
> But Glasclune the deceiver
> Made free wi' a firework
> Tae blaw up his neebor.[3]

I can see Janet walking up the track with her small son and telling him the tale as they glimpsed the castle ahead of them...

And, of course, Glenshee is in the poetry as well:

> Spring quickens. In the Shee Water I'm fishing.
> High on whaups mountain time heaps stone on stone.
> The speech and silence of Christ's world is Gaelic,
> And youth on age, the tree climbs from the bone.[4]

Hamish was a resident of Edinburgh from the early 1950s till his death in 2002. But when he died, his ashes were taken, as he had requested, and laid on the summit of Ben Gulabin. A moving account of the ceremony that day is given by Dr Timothy Neat in the second volume of *Hamish Henderson: A Biography*,[5] and I am indebted to Tim for some of the information in this article.

Next time you are in Blairgowrie – and everyone must go to Blairgowrie! – call in at the Branch Library where you will be greeted by a fine bust of Hamish. This is the work of the sculptor Anthony Morrow and was commissioned by Blairgowrie, Rattray

---

[3] Hamish Henderson, Collected Poems and Songs, p.140.

[4] Hamish Henderson, 'Ballad of the Twelve Stations of My Youth', Collected Poems and Songs, p.23.

[5] Timothy Neat, *Hamish Henderson: A Biography. Vol II: Poetry Becomes People (1954-2002)*, Edinburgh: Birlinn, 2009, pp.364-65.

and District Local History Trust, with the support of the National Lottery. So, Hamish still has a presence in the town of his birth while his mortal remains rest on the hill of legend overlooking his second home in Perthshire, the cottage by the Shee. He is back in Perthshire where he belongs.

EARLY YEARS

This was Blairgowrie' High Street as it was in the early 20s when Hamish was a young boy.

'Drumly Ericht' Hamish called the river which here passes a mill before it reaches Blairgowrie. All the mills are now closed.

The Spittal of Glenshee where Hamish and his mother lived for five years in a rented cottage. Above it rises Ben Gulabin where Hamish's ashes were scattered.

For much of its course the Lornty Burn runs under a canopy of trees. The young Hamish explored its banks with his friend Neil.

All the old postcards are from the collection of Maurice Fleming.

The Berryfields O Blair

Belle Stewart (1906-1997)

When berry time comes roond each year
Blair's population's swelling,
There's every kind o picker there
And every kind o dwellin.
There's tents and huts and caravans,
There's bothies and there's bivvies
And shelters made wi tattie-bags
And dug-outs made wi divvies.

There's corner-boys fae Glesgae,
Kettle-boilers fae Lochee,
There's miners fae the pits o Fife,
Mill-workers fae Dundee
And fisherfolk fae Peterheid A
nd tramps fae everywhere
Aa looking fir a livin aff
The berry fields o blair.

There's travellers fae the Western Isles,
Fae Arran, Mull and Skye;
Fae Harris, Lewis and Kyles o Bute,
They come their luck to try.
Fae Inverness and Aberdeen,
Fae Stornoway and Wick
Aa flock to Blair at the berry time
The straws and rasps to pick.

There's some who earn a pound or twa,
Some cannae earn their keep,
There's some wid pick fae morn till nicht,
And some wid rather sleep.
There's some wha has tae pick or stairve,
And some wha dinnae care,
There's comedy and tragedy
Played on the fields o Blair.

There's families pickin for one purse,
And some wha pick alane,
There's men wha share and share alike
Wi wives wha's no their ain.
There's gladness and there's sadness tae,
There's happy herts and sair,
For there's some wha bless and some wha curse
The berry fields o Blair.

Before I put my pen awa,
It's this I would like to say:
You'll travel far afore you'll meet
A kinder lot than they;
For I've mixed wi them in field and pub
And while I've breath to spare,
I'll bless the hand that led me tae
The berry fields o Blair.

'The Provost was all for it':
The Blairgowrie Festivals, 1967-1970

Jim Bainbridge

In August 1967, a motley crew of Tyneside musicians headed north to a traditional music festival which would live long in our memory, and these words are a reflection, 45 years later, of that very influential weekend of music. One of our number, John Lincoln (known as the 'phantom fiddler'), and my sister Kath had, in 1966, been to the first of the five 'festivals o' Blair' and their glowing reports made the rest of us very keen not to miss 1967.

I had been at college in London until 1966, and been seriously impressed by the 'Stewarts of Blair' at Rod and Danny Stradling's excellent traditional folk club at the 'Fighting Cocks' pub in Kingston-on-Thames. The very presence of the Stewarts was, of course, a major influence, but the actual choice of Blairgowrie as a venue must be credited to one Hamish Henderson – the presence of many other travellers and singers in the area for the berry picking being another reason. My sister Kath was a regular at Edinburgh University Folk Club at the time, and had met Blair festival (and TMSA) founders Pete Shepheard, Jimmy Hutchison and 'young' Davey Stewart at the 1966 Keele festival and later at St Andrews 'Star' folk club. This was the start of a link between that club and our own, the Marsden Inn in South Shields which, even if the clubs are no more, has lasted on a personal level until 2012, and still thrives.

So, that is the background to why we headed north that summer weekend, rather than south to Margate in our anoraks or to San Francisco with flowers in our hair, and this is just an outsider's view of what we found there, and not by any means a history of its origins. So, careless of the expense of the 21 shillings for a weekend all-in ticket and petrol at 2/6 a gallon, I started the 200 mile trip on my Lambretta scooter; John Lincoln went on his own (with fiddle strapped on his back), and Jim Irvine (whistle and spoons) and Trevor Sheridan (banjo) went in the luxury of Jim's Mini over the

Carter Bar for the weekend. We camped by the river, and survived on scotch pies, fish and chips and chocolate bars (not much pub grub in Scotland in those days, you would be lucky to get a bag of crisps). However, simply to hear the Stewarts on home ground was sufficient compensation and, although we had heard recordings of Willie Scott and Jimmy McBeath, it was still an absolute revelation to hear the cream of the real Scottish tradition, very much at home in their own backyard.

We had heard some of the songs and singers before on LP, but the contrast between the sterility of those recordings and the vibrancy of the same songs in their context was so powerful that it has stayed with me all my life, and for me, all the twenty-first century's technology can never match that experience. The fact was that the folk we heard did not really know they were 'folk' singers, had very little to do with the 'folk' revival, and were very much singing and playing for their 'ain folk' in their own community, with no hang-ups about whether the material was 'folk' or not – a valuable lesson.

The very idea of running a festival, at the suggestion of Hamish Henderson, in a fairly conservative town like Blairgowrie at a time when pubs closed at 10pm is surprising on reflection but, in the words of organiser Pete Shepheard. "the provost was all for it", and the precedent for a form of late licensing lay in the annual Braemar night shindig held in the town after the famous Highland Games. So, each night the pubs duly closed at 10, then re-opened at 10.30 for some of the most memorable ceilidhs I have ever been to. I well remember Hamish Henderson (glass of Glenmorangie in hand) discussing the weekend with Karl Dallas in the street outside the Victoria pub and, as the years pass, we realise how much we owe to the vision of that one man.

It is hard, 45 years on, to distinguish one year from another, as they were all pretty special, and at this stage I cannot be sure who was there in which year, so the following memories could be anytime in 1967-70. However, the sheer enjoyment of the music, as well as such non-musical gems as the semi-abusive banter between 'old' Davy Stewart and his long term rival Jimmy McBeath is an abiding memory. There were few folk 'performances', it being more of a town-sized ceilidh (in the true Scots Gaelic sense of a gathering) with a real sense of community and fun to go with the tremendous music. It was a revelation to hear the legendary Jeannie Robertson for the first time, while the Stewarts were well to the fore. Alex was often in full Highland dress, to go with the pipes, and some very rude jokes from the elegant Belle went with her wonderful songs, but truly I had never heard any singing to compare with that of Jane Turriff of Fetterangus, while Campbeltown's Mitchell family and their 'Hame Fareweel' fairly bowled us over.

Mary Brooksbank we had heard of via her 'Jute Mill Song', which was already a folk club favourite (via, I suspect, Ray Fisher?), but its real meaning was all the more incisive when we met this wee Dundee millworker and heard her trenchant Marxist views. I do not know what we expected of the weekend

many folk from south of the border think Scottish music was (and may still be?) mainly bagpipes and Andy Stewart. Now, I think we knew better than that, but the sheer power of this tradition really took us by storm, and when our own music sessions were visited by some of these wonderful people, it was a real bonus. Davy Stewart could never grasp my name and, in the pub sessions, often called on Jimmy Brainbox for a tune, and another abiding memory is of him singing 'I am a Miller tae my trade' in the small room at the Victoria Hotel, while replicating the sound of the mill with his hand and elbow on a formica table, and not realising his hand was bleeding profusely. He could also play jigs with his hand on his cheek – do not ask, I cannot explain, you would need to have been there and seen it.

We played our own music in the small room in the 'Vic', and occasionally on the stairs if the pub was full, but also in the Plough at Rattray, over the river Ericht, where we camped and were assailed by a billion midges, although we were later rescued and invited to stay in real beds by a hospitable local man called Bert. The Stewarts came into the Plough one day, and after some stunning singing from Belle, Cathie and Sheila in that tiny room, Alex followed on with his wonderful pipe marches, and we realised why the pipes were designed for outdoor use! John 'Hoddan' MacDonald, the Lewis bus driver, was another new experience, with his Gaelic singing, while a young Shetland fiddle player called Alistair Bain was allowed to join in with us. As we would now, we always made room for other musicians, but lest you think I view all this through the proverbial rose-coloured specs, I do recall listening to a great traveller singer (whose name escapes me) singing the 'Rigs o' Rye' beautifully in such a session, and his being drowned out by a loud shanty singer and chorus. He eventually gave up, and we gently asked the chorus why it had happened, only to be told – "Ewan

MacColl says he's the best shanty singer in Scotland". Would it happen now? Maybe it would, sadly.

Another memory is that the Northern Ireland Troubles were erupting in that period, and we did not really know what a 'Fenian' tune was, so, innocently playing our music for the Scots-Irish travellers in the Ericht Hotel, our failure to play the 'right tune' in the pub ended in a melee, with ashtrays flying and us beating a puzzled retreat. Having said that, I recall very little trouble of any kind. Our own music was generally better received than it had been in the Ericht, and we played for the dancing at the Wellmeadow stage with the Mona Stewart Ceilidh Band, the late John Mason being her lead fiddle. Mona is still singing and playing piano down in Newton Stewart, incidentally, and John, of course, came to lead the Scottish Fiddle Orchestra with some style. Other memories include Ted Furey, father of the Fureys of Dublin, sitting in the Wellmeadow at 9 a.m after a late night session, waiting with his fiddle for the next tune. It was another revelation that he and Davy Stewart greeted each other as old pals, having busked the fairs and markets of Ireland together many years before.

After the 1967 festival we met, via folk club connections, Finbar and Eddie Furey and Christy Moore, and they went up with us in 1968. Christy still remembers seeing Davy Stewart busking in a shop doorway in Coupar Angus on the way north, but is less clear about the time when he, myself and Trevor Sheridan busked outside Woolworths in Blair and were moved on by the 'polis'. The 'polis' told us we would do better up the street, and he was right.

Davie Glen of Angus, the heavily bearded diddler, kilt wearer and Jew's harp specialist, was a real 'one-off', and to actually meet the great Tom Anderson of Shetland knocked our socks off!

One controversial TMSA decision led to the introduction of competitions in 1968. This was continuing the conscious parallels with the Irish fleadh, the idea being to attract an element of singers and musicians who would not attend a pub session but might go to a competition. I shall leave it to others to judge its success over the years but, personally, I had resolved to stay out of it in 1968. To no avail. I was located and dragged out of the 'Vic' to compete, as there were no entrants for melodeon. I duly won, and missed most of an excellent session – but, as valuable compensation, I now can treasure a winners' certificate, signed by Tom Anderson, even if the competition was a little sparse!

Looking back on those days, a lot of those weekends are a blur, but the whole community 'feel' of it is still the over-riding memory.[1] I think the 'stars' got a pound a day and their keep, and while that basic principle still applies at most TMSA events (I think?) we are all more world-weary now, and the issue of dozens of CDs per week can never be a substitute for a live performance of the 'Dowie Dens of Yarrow' by a traveller who 'had it from the family'. I know some TMSA committees are well aware of this, and try hard enough to retain the best of the past and the tradition we all experienced, (or even lived?) in those days, while moving with the times, although sometimes, in the latter case, maybe only to please funding sources? However, to be fair, we do all live in a very different world, where there are University degrees in folk music, and people make a living (mostly with difficulty) out of the music. It is hard to reconcile all that with Blair 1967 and the sheer joy of it all but, above all else, we 'Border Lowpers' learned that the community aspect of tradition is crucial – it is not just songs and music, there is a lot more to it than that, and we would all do well to remember that fact, especially those who now have any teaching responsibility.

The Blairgowrie festivals came to an end in 1970 and, at a crucial time for the TMSA, were rescued by the late lamented John Watt, a founder member who proudly carried TMSA card No 2, and who successfully moved the whole shebang to Kinross for several more years in 1971. He later, as the 'Muchty Megastar', liaised with another Blair original, Citty Finlayson, to set up the Auchtermuchty

---

[1] Of course, there is, as an *aide memoire*, the LP which Bill Leader recorded that weekend in 1968: 'Festival at Blairgowrie' – on which, alongside Jeannie Robertson. Belle Stewart, Davy Stewart, Mary Brooksbank, Willie Scott and John 'Hoddan' MacDonald, to our surprise, our Marsden Rattlers' version of 'Puppet on a String' appeared (Topic LP 12T181, 1968, now out of print). Bill Leader, the man who recorded many important traditional performers for early Topic LPs, arrived in Blair in 1967 and recorded several live sessions, including the Sunday night ceilidh at the Angus Hotel. Whether our band should have been included on the LP, bearing in mind the company we were in, is debatable, but Bill gave us a couple of tracks. The band had been named after a coal train which ran along the Durham coast from Marsden colliery to the River Tyne, and we had in July been to the Durham Miners Gala. It seemed that every other marching brass band was playing 'Puppet on a String', the latest pop hit from Sandie Shaw (written by Phil Coulter). We liked it and decided to include it in our repertoire. It is still to be heard on that Topic LP among all those great Scots singers, although it has not yet been released on CD.

festival on the principles of the wonderful precedent of Blairgowrie 1966-70, a tradition Jimmy Hutchison follows to this day. The crowds may be at big festivals further south, but for me, the heart of the music still beats strongly in the East of Scotland.

We were so lucky to be at those seminal Blairgowrie festivals, and it comes as no surprise that they have acquired legendary status. As you may have gathered, I had a wonderful time. My only regret is that I missed 1966 and cannot remember why!

Dear Hamish ... Yours Aye, Arthur

Ewan McVicar

Writing about famed North East song collector Gavin Greig In a chapter of his 1981 book *A Grain Of Truth,* journalist Jack Webster gave a snapshot view of Arthur Argo, born in Aberdeen in 1935:

> Of the large family circle, my cousin, Arthur Argo, who became a producer with the BBC, had acquired the closest affinity with the mood and spirit of our great-grandfather's work. Folk song, in fact, had a lean period, but Arthur Argo, with his inherited interest, was there at the beginning of the modern revival. In 1961, while in his mid twenties, he had taken leave of absence from his job as a reporter on *The Press and Journal* to tour the clubs and campus lands of the United States with not much more than a toothbrush, a guitar and a good Scots tongue. In the rovings of his six-month adventure he gathered friends and admirers with names like Bob Dylan, whose legendary status was still in the future. Back home, Arthur was already playing his major part in a folk revival, befriending young lads like Billy Connolly and Gerry Rafferty, and becoming in his own day one of Scotland's leading authorities on the subject of folk music.

Jack does not mention Arthur's role in the founding in 1962 of the Aberdeen Folk Club, his enticing of young fiddling virtuoso Aly Bain down from Shetland to the Central Belt, his encouragement of singer and actress Barbara Dickson at the start of her career, his friendship and work with Jean Redpath, Archie Fisher, and many others, including Hamish Henderson.

Writer, singer, storyteller and songwriter Sheila Douglas has researched a so far unpublished biography of Arthur Argo, and for this purpose got copies from Hamish of Arthur's letters to him. That material is the basis of this piece. Many of Arthur's letters give the day of writing, not the date, so I have ordered them as best I can.

They offer snapshot views of Arthur's developing interest, enskilling and action in the revitalising of Scotland's folk song heritage, and the depth of the support and encouragement Hamish was giving him.

Arthur and Hamish met in 1952. Sheila Douglas wrote:

> Hamish was installed in the Commercial Hotel in Turriff to continue the fieldwork started the year before, when there came a knock on his door. He opened it to find 'a cub reporter from the Turra squeak' who said his name was Arthur Argo and he was the great-grandson of Gavin Greig. Hamish, who knew about the manuscripts reposing in the King's College archives and about the family, could not believe his good fortune. Arthur was interested in song collecting and asked if he could accompany Hamish on his local recording jaunts. As Hamish observed, 'It isn't everyone who has the luck to go out collecting accompanied by the great-grandson of the greatest collector in the area'.

Later that year Hamish brought Arthur to Edinburgh to record songs from him for the School of Scottish Studies archive, and to sing at the 1952 Edinburgh People's Festival Ceilidh. The 1951 Ceilidh had been a great success, but Henderson wrote in an article that 'the second Ceilidh was an even more resounding success than the first one. The aim was again " to present the finest flower of our folk song tradition", but this time the emphasis was "upon young singers who are carrying on the splendid tradition in its integrity"'.

Other singers included the veteran Barra singer Calum Johnston, the famous Lewis sisters Kitty and Marietta MacLeod, North-east bothy ballad singer Frank Steele, Blanche Wood of Portknockie, and Jimmy MacBeath. The whole evening was in honour of the poet Hugh MacDiarmid's sixtieth birthday. In *Alias MacAlias* Hamish Henderson wrote that 'Arthur Argo... delighted the audience by singing earthy bothy ballads in a boyish treble'. Though aged 17 in 1952, Arthur's voice had not yet broken – possibly because of childhood polio.

In 'Scots Folk-song: A Select Discography,' Hamish Henderson wrote that Arthur Argo 'did a great deal of valuable field collecting in his native Buchan' and, in a review of the *Greig-Duncan Folk Song Collection* Vol. 1, that Arthur had 'acted as energiser and catalyst in the good cause of restoring North-East folk-song to the folk – and particularly to the young.'

Arthur's letters to Hamish begin in 1960. Arthur had been enthused by a song collecting trip to the North-East by American folklorist Ken Goldstein, and had begun himself to record singers, at the same time writing a series of related articles for the *Press and Journal* under the title 'Pilgrims of the Cornkist'.[1]

Hamish lent Arthur a tape recorder and reels of tape from the School of Scottish Studies. Arthur wrote from Elgin, after Goldstein had returned to the USA,

> Dear Hamish, Your new machine is just dandy and already I have made a number of recordings with it – including a couple of songs from an itinerant street musician. My stockpile of tapes is beginning to accumulate satisfactorily with some fine songs and fine singers filling up the reels. I'm hoping to get down to the Festival … and could maybe bring the tapes with me then. If that is impossible, perhaps I should send them. Could you advise me on this?
>
> My contacts with the B.B.C. are also working out fine. I have been in Aberdeen recording four small pieces as introduction to four field recordings I made some time ago [though the new recorder is of superior quality Arthur had already been making recordings of broadcastable quality] and these will be broadcast within the next few weeks I understand. They also seem sold on the idea of a half hour programme for Scottish Home Service about my safari with Ken Goldstein.

Arthur hopes Hamish can assist with copies of Goldstein's recordings, and shares with Hamish his excitement at what he is achieving, the richness of what he is finding, and his need for guidance and support.

> You know, Hamish, with the contacts I have already established and the work that obviously demands doing

---

[1] These articles are republished, along with a listing of the recordings made by Arthur that are held in the School of Scottish Studies archives, and a CD of some of these recordings, by Gallus Publications in a 2012 book to mark fifty years of the Aberdeen Folk Club, which was co-founded by Arthur.

with them, I could keep myself in a permanent job for years. Every singer seems to know of four more and a follow-up in such circumstances just adds to the tally.

It is a great pity that Ken has gone. Now, I have no-one within reasonable access to discuss the subject with, to compare notes with and experiences and generally to learn from. Still, I'll just have to educate myself to the best of my abilities.[2]

Another 1960 letter, the only one of Arthur's to be included in *The Armstrong Nose: Selected Letters of Hamish Henderson*, reports on his collecting trips.

I had a couple of days in Leven where I did some recording with Jean [Redpath] and her parents. Her father plays dulcimer and her mother seems to have quite a deal of folk-lore. Unfortunately, I had not the time to make any sort of survey of her repertoire. [These 23 Redpath family recordings are available on the Kist O Riches website. Hamish seems to have quickly followed Arthur's lead, and recorded another 53 items from the Redpath family a couple of months later.]

In Aberdeen I made a flying visit to Jeannie [Robertson] – there I got her daughter [Lizzie Higgins] to sing My Bonnie Bonnie Boy and Bonnie Bogieside – and when I got home I paid a flying visit to Lucy [Stewart] and to Willie Robbie. Didn't get a chance to go past and see Jimmy [MacBeath, probably in Portsoy]. Time just seemed to fly away. Have you made any progress with his tangled web of contracts?

Another example of how problems arising from stipulations and restrictions made in the contracts drawn up by collectors, promoters and record companies create trouble for traditional singers appears later in this letter.

One thing I want to bring to your notice. Peter Kennedy has done to Lucy [Stewart of Fetterangus] what he did to John McDonald [known as The Singing Molecatcher] – got her under contract at two guineas for THREE songs. And again

---

[2] Hamish Henderson, *The Armstrong Nose: Selected Letters*, edited by Alec Finlay, Edinburgh, 1996, p. 101.

there is this ten year clause. [The clause restricted her from recording singing, or maybe even from singing, the songs for the next ten years without Kennedy's permission. While Peter Kennedy's collecting work and BBC broadcasts were of crucial value to the Folk Song Revival, he is still heavily criticised for some of his business actions.] Perhaps you could let me know what you think of this. I told Lucy I would consult you and let her know what you thought. To me, two guineas does not seem a lot for three songs especially with this ten-year-clause.

Arthur's next letter records a brief North-East visit by English singer and entrepreneur Roy Guest, at the time very influential in the developing Edinburgh folk scene.

Actually, I went through to Aberdeen on Sunday to see the Roy Guest show and ended up doing a few songs with him. He came up to Elgin on Monday and saw John McDonald, Pitgaveny. Also, I introduced him to one or two songs. Generally, we had quite a lot of fun so thank you very much indeed for sending him along. I'm most grateful.

Glad you will be able to get around to the recordings I want... Naturally I was very interested to hear about the Schools' records. Finances permitting – and I think they just might – I'd be most interested in getting copies, especially since it will be your great field recordings. Having heard some of them, I know they will be well worth the outlay.

Quite honestly, the idea of sitting down to compile a list of the songs I have on tape appals me but if it will be of any help to you I will be most willing to do so. Anything for the cause!

To a certain extent I have concentrated on the Spey Bay area – Elsie [Morrison] should be back early next month – and have found several other singers and leads to singers in that district. Got several odds and ends of children's lore, the Gaberlunzie Man, and The Bleacher Lassie among others.

The next letter begins with Arthur's distress at the news of a Goldstein family tragedy. He then says he is sending Hamish copies of the *Press and Journal* articles.:

I hope you like them. If you do, perhaps it might be a good point to drop a line to the Editor saying you were glad to see them. Might encourage them to use some more in the future. Naturally it would be inadvisable to say I suggested this!! Since they appeared in the P and J incidentally I've had several letters from interested readers who are going to give me what material they can.

The six *P&J* articles of 31 May to 6 June 1960 were indeed followed later in the year by three more, on 17, 21 and 22 June.
   Arthur continues with news of a recording mishap:

The tapes I made with Elsie Morrison would be no use to you because they were made under atrocious conditions. That's obvious from the results. Her budgie was cheeping like mad, I did cover it up without success, and her relations kept wandering in and out. However, that will only be the first of what I hope should prove to be many visits so I will have better tapes later. [Hamish had already in 1956 recorded 63 items from Elsie Morrison.]

About 140 of Arthur's 1960 and 1961 recordings are in the School of Scottish Studies archive, but many more invaluable recordings and linked material were lost in a fire in his Glasgow flat in 1981, the same year that he died. A late 1961 letter from Elgin indicates something of the quantity of recordings Arthur was gathering, and heralds his approaching six month performing tour of the USA.

Amid a million and one other jobs, I've finally got round to listing tapes. Here are first ten sides with another ten to follow tomorrow. Sorry for the delay. What will be the position about getting them or copies back? ... Phoned K. Goldstein in sheer desperation. He's going to meet me at Idlewild so I'm more at ease in my own mind.

Next comes a 'hurried note' addressed from Hatboro, Pennsylvania:

Jean Redpath was with the Goldsteins at the airport to meet me and that too made a great difference. For at least part of my trip, Jean and I are going to team up so it should be great fun. She has made a tremendous impression over here by the way and is very highly thought of. Not without reason may I add. To me she's really a great singer and is getting even better all the time.

Right now I'm in New York where I am continually bumping into 'folk' folk. By the way, your name alone is quite a pass-word among the people here. Many were asking why you have never toured here. Naturally, I've added to the already high regard in which you are held by telling of your contribution. Reckon you'd be a tremendous hit were you to visit the USA.

Arthur later sends a longer letter from 'Ken's place – Friday'. It begins with comments on Hamish's researching of one of Arthur's songs, probably 'The Lobster', on his about to be released album of 'blue' songs, 'A Wee Thread O' Blue', as Vol. 2 of *Lyrica Erotica* on the American Prestige label.

Seems you've been having yourself quite a time following hard in the footsteps of every clue to the Wee Wee Pot. It was quite fascinating to hear the various stages of the quest; somewhat reminiscent of Jason's search in the Argo for the Golden Fleece. Only this was Hamish's quest for Argo. The test pressing of the album is now out and I am reasonably happy with the result.

Arthur and Jean Redpath parted travelling company. She went to California.

She's really making quite an impact – little wonder. Me? I'm working away doing quite a lot of singing to schools and clubs. The money is not great but it keeps my head above water.... Spoke to several people on this side who know you and send their regards including Tommy Makem (what a dandy singer) and Liam Clancy. Gather from Ken that Dominic [Behan] is coming this way in about a fortnight. Don't know who's going to go under first – Dominic or New York. Certainly they can't both go unscathed. It will be interesting to watch.

Arthur's above query to Hamish about Jimmy MacBeath's 'tangled web of contracts' presages various messages from Jimmy to Hamish via Arthur, seeking advance payment for performances so Jimmy can pay his train fare, anxious appeals for Hamish to arrange more performances, details about a planned performing trip to Dublin Hamish has arranged for Jimmy, conflicts and confusions about performance dates – all passed on and commented upon by Arthur with patient good humour. The messages include an intriguing one in 1962 or so in which Jimmy accepts Hamish's 'invitation to appear in the Folk-Song Show in the Kelvin Hall'. What was this event, apparently in what was a huge performance space more fitted for visits to Glasgow by circuses?

The correspondence of 1962 to 1967 turns to literary matters. First, Arthur sends Hamish a draft of a planned article for US folk magazine *Sing Out.* Then he solicits items from Hamish for *Chapbook* magazine which he and others had started publishing in Aberdeen. Hamish contributed a couple of important pieces to *Chapbook* over its publishing life of five years. The letters of course also include news about singers and performance events, including problems associated with a televised 'Folk Prom'.

In 1964 Arthur is asked to permit a proposed London publication of songs from the Greig-Duncan collection. In his reply refusing permission for use of the material to the editor of this planned work, Arthur incorporates Hamish's support for his concerns about the Anglicisation of the language, unnecessary 'collation' of song text versions, and selected tunes being allocated to collated texts.

Arthur continues to consult Hamish about issues of problematic copyright, details of song texts, book reviews, publications, visiting American performers. In January 1967 there is a flurry of discussion about various matters *re* the edition of *Chapbook* which featured Hamish's own songs. There the correspondence ends. In 1968 Arthur got a job with the BBC and he and his family moved south, where he could more easily consult and concert action with Hamish in person.

Challenge and Response:
Elizabeth Stewart and the Fetterangus Stewarts

Alison McMorland

Within the Scottish Folk Song Revival there is hardly an event or development which does not involve the influence, direct and indirect, of Hamish Henderson. The recent publication of *Up Yon Wide and Lonely Glen: Travellers' Songs, Stories and Tunes of the Fetterangus Stewarts told by Elizabeth Stewart*[1] is such a case in point on several fronts. The Stewarts' ancestral roots are deep and honoured, and when Hamish Henderson first visited Geordie Stewart of Huntly looking for old songs he was directed to Fetterangus to visit Geordie's sisters Lucy and Jean, and his brother Ned saying "That they were weel-kent for their music and songs an the ballads that he wis lookin for." Elizabeth recalls that

> This wis aboot 1955 when I wis jist a quinie aboot sixteen years aul. It's true the family were kent for their music aaready but little did we realise that this tall, slim and quite guid-lookin stranger wis tae tak oor name beyond Aiberdeenshire an so mak it and us weel-kent internationally. This wis tae change oor musical lives forever.

Today Elizabeth Stewart is an outstanding practitioner of the traditional arts; an internationally recognised singer, storyteller, composer, pianist and song writer of remarkable ability who has performed all over the UK and made several tours in America. She is the principal inheritor and advocate of her family, the Fetterangus Stewarts, the Northeast branch of the extended Stewart family of

---

[1] Elizabeth Stewart, *Up Yon Wide and Lonely Glen: Travellers' Songs, Stories and Tunes of the Fetterangus* Stewarts, compiled and edited by Alison McMorland, Jackson, MS: University Press of Mississippi in association with the Elphinstone Institute, University of Aberdeen, 2012.

Travellers in the province of Buchan, the heartland of traditional balladry in Lowland Scotland. This legendary family has had immense musical influence and been visited by musicians, singers, folklorists and journalists over fifty years.

As editor and compiler of *Up Yon Wide and Lonely Glen* I never anticipated the challenge of editing and compiling such a book or the response needed to bring this book into being, and I have to remember the beginnings and background for such an undertaking. When I visited Elizabeth in 1998 at her home in Mintlaw she had quite recently returned from her final singing trip to the USA. I was oblivious that Elizabeth had come home determined that the songs, tales and lore, life stories and music of her family should be put into a book so "That the way of life and Traveller traditions should not be forgotten." I was unaware of this resolution until she asked if I would help her to do such a book. I was unprepared for this; however, on another visit and in listening to Elizabeth's stories of her legendary and famous great-grandfather Crichie Donald and his sons who were all military pipers, and about her grandparents Aul Betty and Aul Jimmsy, of her mother Jean Stewart and aunt Lucy (who I had met) I felt drawn to do so and agreed to undertake it. Why? Like many other people, I had first visited Lucy in the early 1970s (which was when I also first met Elizabeth). I was encouraged to do so by Hamish Henderson, my mentor and valued friend, for as a young singer I was seeking to find out more about Scots songs and ballads, and I was eager to learn from older singers. Hamish had invited me to visit the School of Scottish Studies where initially he gave me a compilation tape of source singers to listen to and which had been prepared as a teaching resource for students. A track of a particular woman singer shone out. I asked if there were any more recordings of her and this prompted him to search in the basement of 27 George Square, returning with a number of tapes solely of Lucy Stewart. Giving over his study to me as my base for listening I was to spend many hours there over several visits. On hearing these reel to reel tapes of Lucy, I was enthralled and inspired by her direct story-telling style and her strong voice which was at times sweet, haunting and stark. I was overwhelmed by the treasury of songs with their beautiful and rare melodies. They told of legendary and historical happenings, there were love songs with much pain and disappointment, songs of longings and struggles, of defiance and humour – both daft and clever. On these visits, I stayed with Hamish and his charming wife Kätzel, receiving a warm welcome and sleeping in the front room of their Melville Terrace flat. I remember a stack of vinyl records in the corner of the room, one of which was of Lucy Stewart singing eleven ballads. Learning songs and ballads from these sources, the Stewart family music already had a hold on me, and when I visited Lucy Stewart in Aberdeenshire this was an important event for me. Elizabeth's request, so many years later, offered me the prospect of deepening my understanding of traditional singing and ballad style and to learn more of the repertoire of this particular area within its context. It also, importantly, presented the opportunity for me to give something back as well as to give something to the future: to record and document cultural riches that were under threat and to aid Elizabeth, guardian of her family's legacy, to realise her dream of a book on the Fetterangus Stewarts.

Elizabeth Stewart was born on 13 May 1939 at the home of her grandma Aul Betty and grandfather Aul Jimmsy, 14 South Street (Duke St), Fetterangus. From her earliest beginnings she was surrounded by family music and song which was steeped in the Traveller and Buchan culture. At that time her grandparents' settled home was a working croft, consisting of two large cornfields at the end of Duke Street and a large piece of land at the back and side of their house and barn. The land was used as a camping ground by other Travellers, for the Stewarts were known for their music and were like a magnet, drawing them to this area. Elizabeth's grandparents had a family of ten sons and four daughters and, before finally settling in Fetterangus, they had lived the traditional traveller lifestyle of wintering in Aberdeen and travelling in the summer months to well known camping grounds such as Udney, Scotstoun Moor, Hatton o Fintry, even as far as Inverurie, the area where the Battle of Harlaw took place. Once having set up camp, they had to provide for themselves, and Aul Betty would travel around the nearby countryside with a pack on her back, whilst Aul Jimmsy would sell good quality goods, china ware, pots and pans from their carts whilst looking after the family. He would also teach the pipes from this base. However, he came into his own when playing at the annual Games' competitions for piping and playing for the dancing. Their sons followed in the footsteps of their distinguished forebears, becoming military pipers, but other instruments were played – fiddles, accordions, whistle and drums – and, as Elizabeth tells, "Every one o them knew the songs and ballads, especially Aul Betty." The family were proud of their ancestral lineage to the Appin Stewarts, believing in the Royal Stewart linkage which made them staunch Jacobite supporters. The stories about their way of life and the strong bond with the land they travelled are embodied in the songs, music and tales which Elizabeth grew up hearing and absorbing.

Elizabeth's grandma aul Betty

Elizabeth's mother Jean Stewart and her aunt Lucy

Elizabeth's musical influences were from her maternal side and most importantly from her mother Jean, her aunt Lucy and her fiddle playing uncle Ned. Jean was the youngest of the family of fourteen and became a highly regarded and talented musician. She studied piano, attaining twelve certificates from the London College of Music, played the accordion, was a composer and dancing teacher. She had her own family dance band at the age of sixteen and from then onwards was engaged by the BBC to play regularly as a soloist and to accompany the likes of Willie Kemp and John Mearns, amongst others. Jean became a household name and with her brother Ned they formed the original Fetterangus Strathspey and Reel Society. She was also an influential teacher throughout Aberdeenshire and is still fondly remembered by the public who enjoyed her music and by ex pupils who became musicians. Her story as a Traveller lass who achieved so much as a working musician is given testament by the journalist and broadcaster Jack Webster who writes:

> Jean Stewart was a musical legend of my early childhood in the 1930s and beyond. When I finally caught up with her in my youth, it was mainly in her role as dance-band leader

around the village halls of Buchan. Whether it was Mintlaw, Maud, New Deer or Strichen, there she would be on stage, a good looking woman with the striking features of her heritage and a ready smile that lit up her face. Then she would burst into life on her accordion and away we went, dancing in the way we used to dance in those days before Rock 'n' Roll. It was post war of scarcity but there was no scarcity of top-class dance-bands and musicians – and none better than by Jean Stewart, who lingers in the memory like a distant song.[2]

Lucy played an important part in Elizabeth's upbringing, given that Jean was a full time musician, and her children were looked after by their aunt Lucy at home. Elizabeth says:

She was aye there tae put us tae school, jist tae tak care o us, plaiting oor hair an singin aa the time, as soon as we were up, morning, noon and night, jist all day really. Some times she telt us the story o the ballad first an then sung it – and Lucy loved history so there wis these stories tae.

Acknowledged in the family as the one who knew all the songs, aunt Lucy was the major inspiration, although all the near family knew and sang most of the songs and ballads. 'The Butcher's Boy', for instance, was always sung by Elizabeth's mother Jean. Elizabeth absorbed a wide repertoire in early childhood. Hearing tragic murder ballads such as 'The Cruel Mother' alongside 'Peer Wee Jockie Clark' and children's songs and games sung to amuse them, they all became part of this rich repertoire.

Lucy was first recorded by Hamish Henderson in 1955, and he returned on other occasions, bringing with him Peter Kennedy, Alan Lomax and then a young American Fulbright scholar named Kenneth Goldstein. All four folklorists recorded Lucy, but it was Kenny Goldstein who later studied the lore and music of the family in the period of October 1958 to June 1960. One fruitful outcome of this project was his superb LP of *Lucy Stewart, Child Ballads, Volume 1.*[3] Kenny wrote in the introductory note to the album of the warm and generous reception he and his family received and

---

[2] Elizabeth Stewart, *Up Yon Wide and Lonely Glen*, pp. 99-100.

[3] Folkways FG3519.

how "They gave everything and asked for nothing in return"– and this is the spirit and legacy which Elizabeth is proud to be part of. So yet again, through the guiding hand and vision of Hamish Henderson, the impact of the Stewart family's songs and ballads resounded on the emerging Scottish folksong revival. From then on people beat a path to Lucy's door, and some very well known ones at that. Ewan MacColl, Peggy Seeger and Charles Parker were working on their award winning radio documentary *Singing the Fishing* and visited her. Lucy called Elizabeth in to play for them, and she played a boogied-up version of 'The Hills of Bennachie'. From this, 'The Fisher Lassies' song was written, and Elizabeth and Jane were invited to record it in Birmingham on the original radio documentary sound track.

Elizabeth's obsession from early childhood was the piano and, surprisingly, it was Lucy who taught her to play 'Endearing Young Charms' and 'My Aul Wife an Your Aul Wife' on the piano at the age of four. From then on there was no stopping Elizabeth's eagerness to play more and more tunes. She loved the bagpipes and the pipe tunes which her mother would play, as well as favourite marches on the piano and accordion. Her mother would let her sit in on the lessons she was giving so that Elizabeth could learn too, and in this way she "picked up reading music frae her." Such was her enthusiasm to play that she first performed in her mother's dance band at the age of nine. This was the beginning of her apprenticeship in the family dance band when, along with her younger sister Jane, they sang and played all over the Northeast. However, by the age of fourteen Elizabeth became so well known for her playing that she first broadcast in Aberdeen as a soloist. Her programme for this was the classic 'heavy' bagpipe marches with six or seven measures or variations. Elizabeth progressed to leading her own band(s) in various line-ups throughout the following years, playing for dances, functions and weddings. She was also a member of The Fetterangus Strathspey and Reel Society and, when her mother died in 1962, Elizabeth took over her role as pianist for the Society's practices and performances. Elizabeth's musical tastes have been, and are, highly eclectic: from blues, rock and roll to classical. However, her greatest and enduring passion has been for the 'auld sangs' and the 'Stewarts' way o' it'. So much so, that in 1972 Elizabeth was invited to represent the family and their music in the USA – this was to be the first of her visits there. She also did tours in the UK singing at well established folk clubs.

In these preceding paragraphs I have given skeletal outlines of the family and the themes which I had to pursue and flesh out with Elizabeth through our field recordings and from the hand written accounts contributed by her. I revisited, but in more depth and detail, tapes held in the School of Celtic and Scottish Studies Archive – those first recorded by Hamish Henderson, Arthur Argo, Hamish with Peter Kennedy, and the Kenneth Goldstein tapes made in 1959-60, all of which I transcribed and documented. We were given great support and encouragement by Dr Margaret Mackay, then Director, who was to extend this throughout the later stage of preparing the final manuscript. I contacted key people who had memories of the family, like Jock Duncan and Jack Webster, and the American calligraphic artist and song enthusiast Howard Glasser who contributed his tapes and journal entries from his 1963 visit to the family. I was invited to produce Elizabeth's double CD *Binnorrie*, made in 2004 for the Elphinstone Institute's Travellers Project at Aberdeen University. Professor Ian Russell and Dr Tom McKean knew that we hoped to publish a book and were immensely supportive, seeing it as a pre-runner to our venture. Elizabeth chose to record a very personal selection of ballads and songs, including some of her own piano tunes and compositions. Importantly, this highlighted her unique singing style and distinctive piano playing. The challenges were many as I have just described, not least the immense treasure trove of material which seemed to grow and grow as I and we delved deeper, intermittently, throughout an eight year period. However, the next stage was to prepare the final manuscript for submission to a publisher. A Creative Scotland Award allowed me to engage others' skills. Jo Miller transcribed the music of over 150 songs, ballads and fragments, her careful handwritten transcriptions were then edited and turned into what is now seen on the page by Ian Abernethy, which proved to be a great musical partnership. Cal Milligan of the School of Celtic and and Scottish Studies oversaw and organised the complete manuscript, transcribing and editing the narrative as we worked on it together which was then passed on to Elizabeth to read, change and add to. The use of the Department of Celtic and Scottish Studies' facilities were made available to us for the preparation of the manuscript over this three year period. Meanwhile – on a voluntary basis – Geordie McIntyre researched and wrote the song notes along with their associated bibliography and Eric Rice transcribed and set Elizabeth's eight piano compositions. Throughout this three year stage we had to co-ordinate and accomodate to each others' already busy lives whilst I remained at the central hub of the whole work as editor and compiler. Our final goal was reached and the manuscript was submitted to the Elphinstone Institute and University Press of Mississippi to be considered. The material had become a 400 page manuscript, holding more than 150 song texts with their musical scores, song notes and bibliography, 80 photographs, a narrative which gives life stories, anecdotes, 28 traditional tales, lore and riddles, all set within a broad network of cultural practices and social history.

Elizabeth Stewart's personal reminiscences are at the heart of this book. She tells of her ancestral family and of three generations of women, of their lives and musical traditions, and of their story traditions. The family narratives, traditional tales and riddles are interwoven throughout, giving a fascinating portrayal of the Stewart family's repository of stories and lore. A diverse anthology of songs complements the prose, ranging from Stewart versions of classic ballads to comic and music hall songs, parodies and children's rhymes. Some of these ballads and songs are now widely sung, having been first brought to the wider public during the Folk Revival. Documented here, we are again reminded of the Stewart source, and of their kith and kin inhabiting the same area as Gavin Greig and James Duncan, whose *Greig-Duncan Folk Song Collection* was amassed during the early years of the twentieth century. At that time very few of their song informants were Travellers, and so the richness of the Stewart song repertoire illustrates the family's and the Travellers' unique role in the preservation of the music and song tradition of the Northeast. Also included are Elizabeth's own music and ballad compositions, bringing modernity to the anthology and adding to the kist of riches that Elizabeth grew up with. She is keen to stress, "It is not a complete collection as there are many more songs and stories, too many in fact for the book to hold." Elizabeth's wish for her family songs, stories and lore to be available highlights her unswerving conviction and belief in her inheritance. It is a tribute to her people, a Traveller family and to the Traveller way of life as known in her lifetime.

In my role as editor and compiler I was obviously aware that such a tribute was immensely important. However, in my endeavour to fulfil her expectations I realised I would also have to merge my own vision in order to shape the book into an artistic whole. I knew why we were doing it, but who would the reading public be? What areas of interest could it contribute to? These questions as well as my own connections and background served to underpin many aspects of the work undertaken: researching all available archival song recordings, comparing different performances of the same song by two members of the family, pressing Elizabeth with further questions to tease out more details and give a fuller description of what she was talking about, to try and remember other verses for a half remembered song fragment – these examples and more were the procedures we engaged upon in working towards our goal.

Hamish Henderson championed the Scottish Travellers, this marginalised ethnic minority living on the outside of society and shown much prejudice and condemnation. It was Hamish who blazed the trail, discovering the vast riches within their oral traditions and culture. It was Hamish who crossed the border in the 1950s and built bridges for a two-way passage. If only he was here today, how he would cheer Elizabeth's determination to celebrate her culture. Without doubt Elizabeth Stewart comes from a legendary Traveller family of pipers, musicians and singers – from the 1920s until the early 1960s her mother Jean Stewart was a household name in the Northeast of Scotland, known for her dance bands, broadcasting and teaching – and her aunt Lucy's ballad singing and treasury of songs made an impact on the 1950-60s Scottish Folk Revival, reaching well beyond these shores.

The influence of these women is still reverberating today and they in turn owed much to their mother Aul Betty, whose own story of a hardworking and resourceful Traveller shows that songs and singing enriched her life and were part of the legacy she left to the family. This book is Elizabeth Stewart's legacy for future generations – and for us all.

Elizabeth and Alison singing the 'Plooman Laddies' of her grandma aul Betty at Cullerlie Singing Festival 2011

Anzio Pipe Band

Pino Mereu
Tom Hubbard

Anzio Pipe Baund

In memoria di
Hamish Henderson (1919-2002)
Eric Fletcher Waters (1913-1944)

per Roger Waters

per chi non ha mai conosciuto
il proprio padre.

Il realismo è solo un mezzo ma
il vero fine è la poesia
Charlie Chaplin

In memory of Hamish Henderson (1919-2002) & Eric Fletcher Waters (1913-1944)
For Roger Waters

In remembraunce o
Hamish Henderson (1919-2002)
Eric Fletcher Waters (1913-1944)

Ti Roger Waters

Fir thir folk wha hae never kent
their faither

Realism's juist a means but
the true end is poetry
Charles Chaplin

for those who have never known their father.
The realism is just a means but the true end is poetry, *Charlie Chaplin.*

Lo sbarco di Anzio da parte delle truppe alleate avvenne il 22 gennaio del 1944.
Le truppe americane erano situate sulla spiaggia di Nettuno mentre quelle britanniche (in prevalenza le divisioni formate da soldati scozzesi) sul litorale di Anzio.

Roma era a circa qualche ora di marcia. Churchill era arrabbiato perché gli americani volevano aspettare per ricongiungersi con il grosso delle truppe e quindi cercare di evitare il più possibile perdite durante l'attacco decisivo, mentre per lui non bisognava perdere tempo. Le notizie che giungevano da Roma riportavano che gran parte dei reparti nazi-fascisti erano stati contagiati dalla sifilide.

Quindi si riteneva quello il momento per attaccare; le truppe tedesche impegnate su tutta la linea Gustav (da Anzio al Sangro) erano poche e male armate. Il mancato attacco e la decisione di aspettare diede la possibilità alle truppe tedesche di ricevere nuovi rinforzi e le truppe subirono numerosi bombardamenti da parte dei caccia e della artiglieria tedesca.

Oltre quattro mesi di guerra sul litorale di Anzio, l'antico porto di Roma che diede i natali a Nerone e Caligola.

Le truppe britanniche solo il 1 di giugno del 1944 riuscirono a riprendere la marcia verso Roma e vi entrarono trionfando al suono delle cornamuse della Anzio Pipe Band il 5 di giugno .

The Anzio landing of Allied troops took place on January 22, 1944. The American troops were situated on the beach of Nettuno while the British troops (mainly the divisions formed by Scottish soldiers) were on the coast of Anzio. Rome was about a few hours of travel away. Churchill was angry because the Americans wanted to wait to be reunited with the bulk of their troops and then try to avoid possible losses during the decisive attack, while he did not want to waste time. The news that came from Rome reported that most nazi-fascist detachments were infected with syphilis. So he

*The Anzio laundin o Allied troops tuik place
on 22 Januar 1944.
The American troops wis stationed on the strand o
Nettuno while the British troops (mainly the division
formed bi Scottish sodgers) wis on the coast o Anzio.*

*Rome wis a wheen oors awa on the merch. Churchill wis
fair bleezin because the Americans wantit ti byde ti be
reunitit wi the feck o the troops and there ettle
ti avoid possible losses durin the decisive attack,
while he didnae want to daidle. In the news
frae Rome it wis reportit that the maist o the
Nazi-fascist detachments wis smit wi syphilis.*

*Sae he thocht this wis the richt moment ti attack: the
Gerry troops wis taen up wi bein on board the Gustav
(frae Anzio ti Sangro), and there werenae aa that mony o
thaim and no weill-airmed. The attack failed and the decision
ti byde gien the Gerries the opportunity ti tak in new
reinforcements and the British tholed plenty bombardments
bi Gerry fechters and artillery.*

*Ower fower months o the war tuik place on the coast
o Anzio, the auncient port o Rome that wis the
birthplace o Nero and Caligula.*

*It wis anerlie on 1 June 1944 that the British troops succeedit
in resumin the merch ti Rome, and they entered it in triumph
ti the soond o the bagpipes o the Anzio Pipe Baund
on 5 June.*

---

thought that was the moment to attack, the German troops being engaged across on board the Gustav (from Anzio to the Sangro), and they were few and poorly armed. The attack failed and the decision to wait gave the German troops the opportunity to receive new reinforcement, and the British troops suffered numerous bombings by German fighters and artillery. Over four months of the war took place on the coast of Anzio, the ancient port of Rome that gave birth to Nero and Caligula. Only on 1 June 1944, the British troops were able to resume the march to Rome, and they entered it in triumph to the sound of the bagpipes of the Anzio Pipe Band on 5 June.

INTRODUZIONE

Acqua , madre, atomo...

Lontano puoi volgere il tuo sguardo ma quel che rimane
impresso nei tuoi occhi è solo quel che accade a te vicino.
Anche gli echi lontani di suoni e parole sono solo un
contorno vuoto e inspiegabile.

Non vedo più Barney Bree – fino a qualche minuto fa
suonava la cornamusa, – il suo tema preferito...

hi hiò tra endrè hi horò rò en dum

E ora solo polvere , scoppi, urla, e odore di carne, bruciata,
lacerata, straziata, vite perdute, amori infranti, sogni e
speranze negate.

Quando arriverà il silenzio? La pace?
Dentro di noi e fuori, anche lontano da qui.
Per un momento, per un attimo.

Ecco, ora il silenzio, posso chiudere gli occhi
anche per un solo istante e
tornare a respirare.

Introduction/ Water, mother, atom ... / Far you can turn your eye, but what lingers in your eyes
is just what's happening near you. Even the distant echoes of sounds and words are empty
and an outline, unexplained./ I can no longer see Barney Bree – until a few minutes ago he was
playing the bagpipes – his favorite tune .../ hi hiò tra endrè hi horò rò en dum/ And now only

INTRODUCTION

Watter, mither, atom ...

Ye can look faur, but whit bydes lang in yer een is juist
whit's goin on near ye. Forby the faur aichoes o soonds
and words are empty, an ootline ainly
ayont oor ken.

I canna see Barney Bree ony mair – juist a puckle minutes
syne he wis pleyin the pipes ... his favourite tuin ...

Hi hiò tra endrè hi horò rò en dum

And nou there's juist stour, explosions, skreichs, the smell
o flesh, brunt, rent, riven, tint lives, smattert loves, dreams,
and hopes nae-said.

Whan will silence come? Peace?
In – and oot-by us, forby faur frae here.
In a glisk, in a blink.

Nou, though, the silence, I can shut my een
even fir wan wee moment and
aince mair breathe free.

---

dust, explosions, screams and the smell of meat, burned, torn, lost lives, broken loves, hopes
and dreams denied./ When will the silence arrive? The peace?/ Inside and outside of us, even far
from here./ For a moment, for a instant./ Here, now in silence, I can close my eyes/ even for a
moment and breathe freely again.

Anzio, 44

il mio nome è Seamus tenente della
centocinquantaquattresima
brigata della cinquantunesima Divisione delle
delle Highland ma per loro il poeta dannato.

Vivo mentre la morte attende di
compiere la sua incisione e come bastardo
vivo in un anonimo silenzio.

Siamo scozzesi, tutti veniamo da luoghi
vicini – i nostri abiti di guerra identificano
il luogo dove siamo nati, e da dove veniamo.

Terre alte, a nord, terre di pastori, contadini,
pescatori – ora proletari in divisa e gonnellino
venuti qui a portare la libertà –

Una brigata di proletari in kilt, dai colori
delle famiglie delle isole, dal Banffshire o come
me, dal Ross & Cromarty... terre ora lontane.

La sera quando è silenzio attorno a noi,
suoniamo e cantiamo le nostre canzoni – quelle che
abbiamo appreso da piccoli dai nostri genitori.

Ho pensato a mia madre, alla sua voce,
al suo canto, alla sua bellezza. E nonna che
mi sussurrava storie antiche tutto il giorno.

Anzio, 44: My name is Seamus, lieutenant of the one Hundred Fifty-Four Brigade of the Fifty-One Highland Division but for them I am the damned poet/ I live while waiting for death to make his final cut and like a bastard/ I live in an anonymous silence./ We're Scottish, we are all from neighbouring places – our war clothes identify /the place where we were born, and where we came from./ Highlands, northern region, land of shepherds, farmers, fishermen – now proletarians in uniform and kilt coming here to bring freedom –/ A brigade of proletarians

Anzio, 44

Ah'm cried Hamish lieutenant o the
Hunner and fifty-fourt
Brigade o the Fifty-fourt Hielan Division
but fir thaim Ah'm the makar *maudit*.

Ah leeve bydin fir daith ti
feenish his lest cut and like a bastart
Ah leeve in an anonymous seelence.

We're Scottish, aa frae neebourin
airts – oor fechtin claes tell ye
whaur we wis born, whaur we cam frae.

Hielan, up north, laund o herds, fermers,
fisherfolk – nou proles in uniforms and kilts
come here ti bring freedom –

Brigade o proles in kilts, wi the colours
o the faimilies o the islands, or frae Banffshire or like
me, frae Ross and Cromarty ... nou laund faur frae here.

Nichts whan the seelence's aroun us
we pley oor pipes and sing oor sangs – sangs we've
lairnt as bairns frae oor forefolk.

Ah mynd ma mither, her voice,
her singin, its bonnieness. And o ma graundmither
whusperin til 's auld legends the lee-lang day.

---

in kilts, with the colors of the families of the islands, or from Banffshire and, like me, from Ross
& Cromarty ... now a land far from here./ At night when silence is around us, we play and sing
our songs – those that we have learned from our parents and parents' parents when we were
children./ I remember my mother, her voice, her singing, her beauty. And my grandmother who
whispered to me ancient stories all day.

Mio padre è caduto ad Anzio assieme a molti altri suoi compagni. Io ero nato da poco, avevo appena undici mese. Mia madre in realtà non mi ha mai raccontato bene tutta la storia. All'inizio diceva che ero troppo piccolo, poi quando sono diventato grande diceva che non ricordava molto: soltanto che era partito per la guerra per portare la libertà in quelle terre. Era convinto di ciò che stava facendo. Mia madre ad Anzio è andata molte volte con altre donne, chi aveva perso figli, mariti, fidanzati, cugini ma ha sempre pensato che per me sarebbe stato un viaggio troppo lungo e che i ricordi dovevano essere dentro questa casa magari nel vedere una foto e immaginare i tempi in cui lui era felice. Perché ci sono stati. Come quando ha ricevuto la notizia che ero nato e la sua gioia di potermi abbracciare. Ma non lo ha mai potuto fare. Anzio, sul mare a 40 chilometri da Roma, Italia.

My father died at Anzio together with many of his comrades. I was a baby; I was just eleven months old. My mother never really told me the whole story. At first she said that I was too young to understand, and then when I was grown up she did not remember much: only that my father had left home for the war to bring freedom to our homeland. He believed in what he was doing. My mother went to Anzio many times with other women who had lost sons, husbands,

My faither deed at Anzio thegither wi mony o his comrades. I wis a baby, juist eleeven month. My mither never really telt me the haill story. At first she said I wis ower wee ti unnerstaund, then whan I growed up she didnae mynd o muckle: juist that my faither left hame fir the war ti bring freedom ti thae hamelaunds. He believed in whit he wis daein. My mither gaed ti Anzio mony times wi ither women wha had tint sons, husbands, cleeks, cousins, but she aye thocht that it wad hae been a lang trip fir me and that it wis best ti keep the memories ben this hoose bi lookin at a photie and thinkin aboot the times whan he wis blythe. There were sic times. Sic as whan he heard the news that I wis born and wis fair joco at bein able ti haud me. But he wis never able ti dae thon. Anzio, on the sea, wis forty kilometre frae Rome, Italy.

boyfriends, cousins. She thought that it would have been long a trip for me and that it was best to keep the memories in our home by looking at a photograph and imagining the times when he was happy. Because there were such times. Like when he received the news of my birth, and his joy in being able to embrace me. But he was never able to do it. Anzio, by the seaside, was at a distance of 40 kilometers from Rome, Italy.

Abbiamo respirato e poi tossito tutta questa
polvere mentre la nostalgia e il solo pensiero
alla nostra Europa procurava dolore.

In questa notte pallida le navi ci portano
fuori dalla baia ricoperta di alberi
con le palme, via, lontano .

Addio Salerno queste acque di un mare ora
limpido, si agitano, si increspano e
si oscurano con il lento muoversi delle onde.

Ci prepariamo allo sbarco. Giovani ragazzi,
un po' sbruffoni, stanno pulendo le armi,
scherzando a voce alta

e al finir del canto chiassoso in quel dialetto
si sbarca di notte, ora in silenzio, come ladri
gettati in acqua a pochi metri dalla riva.

We breathed and then coughed all this dust, while the nostalgia and thinking of our Europe
caused pain./ On this night, pale ships take us out of the bay covered with trees, palm trees,
far, far away./ So long Salerno, these waters of a sea now clear, shake, ripple and dim, with the

We breathed and then hoastit aa this
stour while the nostalgie and the anerlie thocht
o oor Europe gien us pain.

This nicht pale-like ships cairry
oot o the bay happit wi trees,
palm trees, faur aff

Fare ye weill, Salerno, thir watters o a sea nou
clear, restless, ripplin and
mirkenin, wi the slaw steirin o the waves.

We're gettin ready ti laund. Young lawdies,
a bit fu o theirsels, are cleanin their wappens,
gien it laldy wi their baurs

and ti feenish the roarin sang in thon speik
we laundit at nicht, nou in seelence, like briganners
flung inti the watter a wheen metre frae the shore.

---

slow movement of the waves./ We are preparing to land. Young lads, little 'braggarts, are cleaning their weapons, joking loudly and to finish the song in that dialect we landed at night, now silent, as thieves thrown into the water a few meters from the shore.

Per cinque lunghissimi mesi furono sotto attacco di caccia bombardieri tedeschi e frequenti attacchi di artiglieria, Anzio era una perfetta zona di guerra: incroci di strade, zona industriale , linea ferroviaria. Mamma tutte queste cose non le ha nemmeno più pensate: ci sono i libri, i racconti di chi è tornato e vuole anche dimenticare, chi è tornato e vuole anche continuare. Ma io voglio forse sapere solo la verità : quel Gesù è crocifisso perché mio padre è morto ?

For five long months we were under attack from German bombers and from frequent attacks of artillery. Anzio was a perfect war zone: intersections of roads, an industrial area, the railway line. All these things Mamma has not even thought about again: there are books, stories of

Fir five lang months we wis unner attack frae Gerry bombers and frequent attacks o artillery. Anzio wis a perfect war zone: intersections o roads, industrial zones, the railway line. Aa thae things Mum hasnae even thocht aboot again: there are buiks, stories aboot aa thir that cam back and juist want ti forget, forby aa thir that cam back and want ti gang on. But mebbe I juist want ti ken the truth: Jesus on the cross whit fir is my faither deid?

those who came back and also wanted to forget, and those who came back and wanted to go on. But perhaps I only want to know the truth: Jesus crucified – why is my father dead?

Phil ride. Lui tornerà dalle sue pecore, laggiù
al suo villaggio. Sposerà la sua bella e tornerà
a parlare gaelico. Dimenticherà tutto.

"Ne ho seppelliti troppi, di compagni". Mi
chiedo cosa farò quando tornerò a casa,
mi sembra di sentire il vuoto.

Hi ha ra dun hò ha ra rin dun tro
Hi ha ra dun hò ha ra rin dun tra

Una piccola banda di suonatori
di cornamusa abbiamo formato,
non solo i Dragons ma anche noi.

Proletari in kilt, barney bree,
Alec, e Phil, Red Neill e
al tamburo, Donnie.

Andiamo a Capri a far baldoria
i faraglioni, la grotta azzurra
le antiche ville sul mare.

Compagni godiamoci brandelli
di sole ormai la luna è sfuggente,
Capri ci attende.

Phil laughs. He will return to his sheep, to his village. Marry his beauty and again speak Gaelic.
Forget everything./ "I've buried too many comrades." I wonder what will I do when I get home,
I seem to feel the void.'/ Hi ho ra dun hò ha ra rin dun tro/ Hi ho ra dun hò ha ra rin dun tro/ A
small band of pipers we formed; no longer just the Dragons but we ourseves./ Proletarians in

Phil lauchs. He'll come back frae 's sheep, doun by
ti his clachan. Mairry his quean and gang back
ti speik the Gaelic. Forget aathin.

'Ah've yirdit ower mony o thaim, ma comrades'.
Ah'm wunnerin whit Ah'll dae whan Ah get hame,
Ah've a notion o the void.

Hi ha ra dun hò ha ra rin dun tro
Hi ha ra dun hò ha ra rin dun tra

A wee baund o pipers
we werenae juist the Dragons
but wirsels forby.

Warkin men in kilts, Barney Bree,
Alec, and Phil, forby Reid Neill and
The drummer, Donnie.

Lat's awa ti a ceilidh in Capri,
The Faraglioni, the Blae Grotto,
the Roman villas on the sea.

Comrades lat's fest wi shreids o
sun, nou the müne hynes awa,
Capri bydes fir 's.

Hinda odrò, hio ò odrò, hinde odrò, chè o chè
Hio è edrè, chè è edrè, hò è odrò, hiorin trò -...

Tutti corrono festanti al suono
di cornamuse sotto il controllo
annoiato degli americani

Per il corso abbiamo suonato
È festa, per questa sera
dimentichiamo l'atroce destino.

Prima di notte la notizia è
giunta senza aspettare, Anzio ci
attende sul lungomare.

Hinda odrò, hio ò odrò, hinde odrò, chè o chè/ Hio è edrè, chè è edrè, hò è odrò, hiorin trò .../
Everybody runs to the party sounds of bagpipes under the bored control of the Americans/ For

Hinda odrò, hio ò odrò, hinde odrò, chè o chè
Hio è edrè, chè è edrè, hò è odrò, hiorin trò

Aabody rins ti the ceilidh
soonds o pipes unner the
pissed-aff control o Yanks

we pleyed fir the corso
it's a ceilidh, fir this nicht
we forget the awfy weird.

Afore nicht the news
has got through, Anzio bydes fir us
alang the shore.

the corso we played/ It is a fiesta for tonight forget the dreadful fate./ Before night the news
has come, Anzio awaits us on the seafront.

The Anzio Pipe Band May 1944: Hamish's pipe band performs for wounded American troops at Nettuno.

© Felicity Henderson

The Anzio Pipe Band May 1944: Hamish's pipe band performs for wounded American troops at Nettuno.

© Felicity Henderson

Che cosa accade? Che cosa abbiamo fatto?
Bandiere di guerra, stendardi.
Cosa posso ricordare? una immagine, un documentario, la
radio che si accende da sola mentre continuo a giocare in
solitudine senza capire nulla.
Che cosa posso ricordare? una lingua intrecciata, una
preghiera terrorizzata totalmente fredda di sentimenti che ti
scorre dentro il sangue.
Che cosa posso ricordare? Qualcuno si ricorda di me?

What happens? What have we done? Flags of war, banners. What do I remember? An image,
a documentary, the radio turns itself on while I continue to play alone without understanding

Whit happens? Whit hae we düne?
Flags o war, banners.
Whit dae I hae in mynd? A picter, a documentary, the
radio turns itsel on while I cairry on pleyin my lane withoot
unnerstaunin onythin.
Whit can I mynd o? A twistit tongue,
a prayer sae completely emotionally frigid that the
bluid rins cauld through ye.
Whit can I mynd o? Dis onybody mynd o me?

anything. What can I remember? A twisted tongue, a terrified prayer sending cold feelings
flowing through your blood. What can I remember? Does anyone remember me?

Quando sentite i nostri fucili
tuonare: è il nostro asso
che cade giù, senza tremare.

Non c è alcun lamento né veglie
né gemiti né urla, abbiamo solo
paura nella mente.

I ragazzi stanno suonando ora *l'assedio
di Delhi*, talmente forte da
rimanere storditi.

Via dalla spiaggia, dal litorale:
tende, carri , è l'ora muoversi
verso Roma.

Sulla linea di Cassino la Divisione piange
sotto le bombe, l'assedio, ma ora
tocca a noi.

Prima linea. Verso casa. Il
Problema è che comincio a pensare di
essere maledetto.

Un poeta maledetto: per Cristo
credetemi, non sbaglio è il
mio maggior problema.

Fuori c'è tutto il resto: l'inferno,
loro – i nemici, ad attenderci e
la morte ostinata.

When you hear our guns thunder: it is our ace falling down, without trembling./ There is no crying nor vigils or groans or screams, we have only fear in our mind./ The guys are playing now The Siege of Delhi, so strong you are stunned./ Away from the beach, from the coast: tents, wagons, it's time to move to Rome./ On line of Cassino the Division groans under the

Whan ye hear wir guns
thunner: hit's wir ace
facin doun, withoot tremmlin.

There's nae greetin nor vigils
nor manes not skreiks, we've ainly
dreid i the mynd.

The boys is pleyin nou *The Siege*
o *Delhi*, that strang
ye byde bumbazed.

Awa frae the strand, frae the shore,
tents, trucks, we're best haudin forrit
ti Rome.

On the line o Cassino the Division murns
unner the bombs, the siege, but nou
hit's up ti us.

First line. Tak me hame.
The problem's I'm stertin ti think
I'm in deep shite.

A makar fuckt up likes: fir bi Christ
there nae mistak, here hit's
my problem big-time.

Ootside, there's aathin else: aa hell,
faes ti expeck and
the dour daith.

---

bombs, the siege, but now it's up to us./ First line. Take Me Home. The Problem is that I start
to think that I am damned!/ A cursed poet: for Christ believe me, I'm not mistaken, this is my
biggest problem./ Outside, there's everything else: the hell of them – enemies, and waiting for
a stubborn death.

Lei, la morte, percuote il suo piccolo
tamburo, la primavera è giunta con
il nostro sangue.

Qualsiasi idea per abbattere quei
giovani virgulti teutonici
sarebbe andata bene.

bisogna stare qui – fermi –
in questa dannata attesa con
il dio del silenzio.

Phil ci ha mostrato il morso del
suo bambino: la posta ha portato foto
e carte truccate;

anche per Donnie, bastardo
fortunato, ma niente per me,
niente di niente.

Her, death herself beats her small drum, spring has come with our blood./ Any idea for cutting
down the young Germans would be good./ You must be here – firm in this damn waiting with

Her, ay, daith herself, beats
her wee drum, the spring forby
has come wi oor bluid.

Ony idea fir hammerin
the young breed o Gerries –
wad hae been graund likes.

But we need ti be here – still –
in this bastardin wait wi
the god of seelence.

Phil shawed us the bite o
his bairn: the mail's brocht photies
and merked cairds

forby fir Donnie, the lucky
bastart, but nae nuthin fir me,
bugger aa.

the god of silence./ Phil showed us the bite of his child: the mail has brought photos and marked
cairds;/ for Donnie, you lucky bastard, but nothing for me, no nothing.

E poi la danza, il canto: le campane della chiesa suoneranno e infiammeranno il mio cuore, la mia memoria. L'altra notte ho fatto un sogno fluttuante tra le nuvole ormai agonizzanti: cercavo un luogo dove stare e abbastanza per mangiare e dove finalmente non posso ascoltare e attendere chi viene a bussare alla porta. Né dubbi, né paure. Nessuno così ucciderà altri bambini. Così notte dopo notte tutto torna a girare attorno alla mia testa fino a rendermi pazzo in una terra straniera dove quel che è stato fatto è stato fatto. Non posso riscrivere il finale, né posso tagliarlo, sebbene sia l'ultimo.

And then the dancing, the singing: church bells will ring and will fire up my heart, my memory. The other night I had a dream of floating in the clouds now dying: looking for a place to stay and enough to eat and where at last I need not to wait and listen to who comes knocking at the

And then the dauncin, the singin: the kirk bells'll ring and fire up my hert likes, my memory. The ither nicht I had a dream floatin amang the cloods nou deein: I wis lookin fir a place ti stey and eneuch ti eat and whaur at lest I dinnae need I listen ti and byde fir whitever comes chappin at the door. Nae doobts, nae fears. Naebody kills the bairns ony mair. Sae nicht efter nicht ti turn aathin back aroun my heid ti mak me gyte in a strange kintra whaur whit wis düne wis düne. I cannae rewrite the endin, though it's the lest ane.

door. Neither doubts, nor fears. And no-one kills the children anymore. So, night after night I turn everything around in my head, to make me crazy in a strange land where what was done was done. I cannot rewrite the ending, I cannot cut it, although it's the last one.

Corre diretto verso Anzio
i tedeschi controllano tutto
nascosti e sicuri

nel loro profondo e confortevole
tunnel con quella artiglieria
da quattro soldi

Enorme distesa di camion a pochi
metri, sotto più sicuri sottoterra
per questa battaglia

A Cassino si cade e si muore.
A Roma i fascisti giacciono
tra soffici lenzuola.

Statale 6 solo un convoglio
avanza verso di noi: è strano
è quasi a tiro.

It runs directly toward Anzio the Germans control everything hidden and safe/ in their deep and
comfortable tunnel with their two-bit artillery/ Huge rows of trucks within a few meters, safest

Hit rins towart Anzio
the Gerries control aathin
hid and safe

i their deep and snod
tonnel wi the artillery
they got fir bawbees

muckle collection o trucks
in a wee area, safer unnergrund
fir this fecht

at Cassino faas and dees.
In Rome, the fascists lee
tween saft sheets.

Statale 6 juist a convoy
haudin forrit til 's: hit's unco
and aamaist in reenge.

underground for this battle/ At Cassino you fall and die. In Rome, the Fascists lie between soft
sheets./ Statale 6 is just a convoy advancing towards us: it is strange and almost in sight.

I primi colpi. In questo cerchio.
I loro caccia lanciano le
prime lordure

decisi a spedirci tutti all'inferno.
in questo spettacolo da macellai
non hanno perso tempo.

Noi come loro. Cerchiamo
di ritirarci da lì. Tredici dei
nostri sono caduti.

Ancora fermi in attesa, dei
nostri aerei con l'inclinazione
ad avanzare.

L'ordine è dato: giù per quel
sentiero, senza tregua, correre
sparare, urlare.

Ad ovest verso i guadi, suoneremo
le nostre cornamuse e i tedeschi
danzeranno con la morte accanto.

Si corre solo per il bruciore che
sentiamo e proviamo, la morte ostinata
percuote il suo piccolo tamburo;

ci sono nascondigli, vie di fuga, assedi,
cannoneggiamenti... da lì giungono
i rifornimenti per strada.

The first shots. In this circle. Their jabos launched the first shit/ decided to send us all to hell in
this show from butchers they wasted no time./ Neither did we. We try to withdraw from there.
Thirteen of us have fallen./ Still stuck on waiting for our planes, with the inclination to advance./
The order is given: down that path, relentlessly, running shooting, screaming./ To the West

The first shots. I this circle
their first settin-efter
launched the first shite

decidit ti send us aa ti buggery
in this butcher's shaw
they werenae daidlin.

Us like thaim. We ettle
ti get oot o there. Thirteen o oor boys
are gone corbie.

Still taigled bydin on
wir planes hotchin fain
ti haud forrit

The order's oot: doun ti that
peth, nae lissance, rinnin
firin, yellochin.

Ti the Wast towart the fuird, we'll pley
wir pipes and the Gerries
will daunce alang wi daith.

Ti rin anerlie fir the brennin sensation
we feel and pruive, daith dourly
chappin her wee-bit drum;

there nae hidin places, escape-routes,
brattle o guns ... comin frae there
supplies fir the road.

---

towards the fords, we'll play our bagpipes, and the Germans will dance with death next./ You
run only for the burning sensation that/ We feel, death stubbornly beats her little drum;/ there
are no hiding places, escape routes, sieges, gunfire ... from there come supplies for the road.

Si corre, si inciampa, si cade in questo
ultimo istante di agonia. Consumati letteralmente
bruciati, sbudellati, colpiti alla gola.

Red Neill fischietta *Tulloch Gorum*.
Poi cade una grossa macchia di
sangue copre il suo stomaco

Nubi di acqua e sangue dal cielo
dichiarazione di imminente tempesta.
E siamo ancora all'inizio...

BOOOUUUMMMMMMMMMM!!!!!!!!!!!

L'assedio di Delhi risuona come un
ronzio nella testa di Phil. Si
addormenterà per sempre.

Run, stumble, fall in these last moments of agony. Consumed, literally, by flames, gutted, shot
in the throat./ Red Neill whistles Tulloch Gorum. Then he drops, a large patch o blood covers
his stomach./ Clouds of water and blood from the sky. Reports of the impending storm. And we

Rin, stumble, faa in this
lest instant o agony. Literally consumed,
brunt, grallocht, shot i the thrapple.

Reid Neill whustles *Tulloch Gorum*.
He draps, a muckle tash o bluid
covers his stammack.

Cloods o watter and bluid frae the lift,
spaein a muckle storm.
and we're still at the beginnin ...

BOOOOOOMMMMMMMMMM!!!!!!!!!!!

The Siege o Delhi dirls like a bizzin
in Phil's heid. He
faas asleep fir aye.

---

are still at .../ BOOOUUUMMMMMMMMMMM!!!!/ The siege of Delhi sounds like a buzzing in the
head of Phil. /He falls asleep for ever.

finalmente posso mettermi una maschera per allontanare
i proiettili, calarmi un elmetto sfidare così la luce del sole,
mirarne i capelli dorati. Posso prendere la fragilità e portarla
in una mano o nasconderla: non c'è più alcuno che ricorre alla
legge. Notte dopo notte ho bisogno di altri sogni. Credere
alla storia di fama fortuna e gloria. Queste mani sono ormai
affondate nella sabbia. Si cresce in casa come in un piccolo
luogo che diventa pian piano un memoriale : il ricordo di un re
che non torna più, che niente tornerà indietro. Solo ricordi di
quel che ci spetta: che ci sia almeno un poco di rispetto. Posso
continuare a giocare nei campi e udire bang bang e scoprire
che sei morto.

I can finally wear a mask to ward off the bullets, put on a helmet to challenge the sunlight,
looking for golden hairs. Can I hold my weakness in my hand or hide it: there is nobody any
longer resorting to the law. Night after night, I need more dreams. To believe the story of fame,
fortune and glory. These hands are now sunk in the sand. It grows at home as in a small place

I can at lest weir a mask ti weir aff the bullets, lat doun a helmet ti haud aff the sunlicht, aimin at gowden hairs. I can tak the weakness and cairry it in ae haund or hide it: there's naebody resortin ti the law ony mair. Nicht efter nicht I need ither dreams. Ti credit the story o fame, fortune and glory. Thir haunds are nou sunk in the saund. It growes at hame like a wee place that slawly becomes a memorial: the memory o a king wha never comes back, forby naethin will come back. Juist memories o whit waits fir us: there's at least a bittie respeck. I can cairry on pleyin in the fields, hear and see bang bang ye're deid.

that slowly becomes a memorial: the memory of a king who never comes back, as nothing will come back. Only memories of what awaits us: there's at least a little respect. I can go on playing in the fields and see and hear bang bang you're dead.

Si può parlare dei compagni del
Moray alla mano e coraggiosi, dei
fucilieri scelti dello Scottish Royal,
fortemente simpatici , ma

qui nella battaglia di Anzio, c'è
da sapere che a tenere la prima
linea ci sono ragazzi di Banff,
i proletari di Scozia

figli di artigiani, contadini, pastori
dell'interno, pescatori della costa
l'uno al fianco dell'altro, uniti come
a difendere le proprie terre.

Chi è stato sconfitto può capire e
comprendere l'errore di non aver stimato
la forza e il coraggio di questi
giovani ragazzi del Banffshire.

Non temono nulla, i loro figli un
giorno leggeranno la storia di Anzio,
di come i loro padri hanno combattuto,
chi è caduto, chi è tornato.

Roma non è stata ancora liberata,
quando vi entreremo sarà la
Anzio Pipe Band a suonare per
non dimenticare nessuno.

One can speak of the companions of Moray, handsome and brave, the Royal Scottish Fusiliers
chosen, very nice, but/ here in the battle of Anzio, it is about knowing how to hold the first
line, there are guys in Banff, the proletariat of Scotland/ sons of artisans, farmers, shepherds,
fishermen of the coast alongside each other, united as if they defended their own lands./ Those
who were defeated understand the error of having underestimated the strength and courage

Ye can talk aboot the comrades o
Moray, jack-easy and brave, o
the wale o the Royal Scottish Fusiliers,
awfy nice, but

here in the battle o Anzio, it's
aboot kennin ti haud the first
lines, there's fellaes frae Banff,
the warkin-men o Scotland.

Sons o skeelie labourers, crofters, herds,
fishers o the coast,
ane aside the ither, aa yin ti
defend their ain laund.

Whaever wis defaitit can unnerstaund
the mistak o unnerestimatin
the strength and saul o thir
young lawdies frae Banffshire.

Dinnae fear, their bairns ae day'll
read the story o Anzio,
o hou their faithers focht,
wha fell, wha come back.

Rome hasnae yit been liberatit,
but whan they mak their entry there,
The Anzio Pipe Baund will pley
Sae naebody's forgot.

of these young boys from Banffshire./ Have no fear, their children, one day, will read the story
of Anzio, of how their fathers fought, those who have fallen, those who have returned./ Rome
has not yet been liberated,/ But when we enter the Anzio Pipe Band will play, so nobody will
be forgotten.

I miei occhi sarebbero ormai di ghiaccio paranoici e ormai lontani mille miglia, nascosti e pietrificati, se almeno questo cielo così azzurro potesse per un attimo rendermi felice. Ombre, spettri, paure di nessun calore e colore: perché non dire una piccola verità? Dove posso nascondermi se mostro sempre il mio lato oscuro, dove posso mostrarmi se ora ho venduto la tua storia, dove posso chiamare se nessuno mi riporta a casa. Dove posso amare se mi sento così nudo con le mani tremanti e se i miei nervi non reggono la scena finale. Fatemi sorridere, piangere, cantare, pregare, ballare, fatemi stare, sentirmi a posto.

My eyes would have become paranoid cold and now thousands of miles away, hidden and petrified, if at least this sky so blue could for a moment make me happy. Shadows, ghosts, fears without heat or colour, why not tell a little truth? Where can I hide if I always show my dark side,

My een wad hae become paranoid cauld and nou thoosan mile awa, hid and petrifeed, gin at least this lift sae blae cuid juist fir a moment mak me blythe. Shaddaes, ghaists, dreids withoot heat or colour, whit fir no tell a wee bit truth? Whaur can I hide gin I aye shaw my daurk side, whaur can I shaw mysel nou I hae telt your story, whaur can I cry oot gin naebody taks me hame. Whaur can I love whan I feel sae bare scuddie wi tremmlin haunds, and gin my nerves cannae face the final act. Mak me smile, greet, sing, pray, daunce, mak me byde easy, feel braw.

where can I show myself now that I've told your story, where can I call if no one takes me home. Where can I love when I feel so bare with trembling hands, and if my nerves cannot face the final act. Make me smile, cry, sing, pray, dance, make me feel, feel alright.

Era già tutto finito. Da tempo – quando abbiamo
iniziato a scavare: dolore, disperazione, strazio, odio
tutto girava attorno a noi: la perdita, il vuoto incolmabile,
l'eccidio, il sacrificio, l'infamia: non potevamo nulla.

Sabbia, pietra, scavare, scavare dentro quella grotta
dare la luce a sempre più poveri corpi, con e senza
nome – all'alba di un nuovo giorno per chi rimane,
chi li piangerà, chi non li dimenticherà. Mai.

It was already over. For a long time – as we started to dig: pain, despair, anguish, hatred
everything revolved around us: the loss, the unbridgeable gap, the massacre, the sacrifice, the
shame: we could do nothing./ Sand, stone, dig, dig, dig into that cave bring to light more and

Hit wis aareadies ower. Fir a time – whan we'd
stertit ti dig: pain, wanhope, fasherie, hate –
aathin birled aroun us: the loss, the owerwhummlin emptiness,
the slauchter, the sacrifeece, the shame: nae remeid.

Saund, stane, dig, dell inti the cave
gie licht ti aye mair puir bodies, wi and withoot
name – at the dawin o a new day fir thir wha byde,
thir wha greet, thir wha winna forget thaim. Never.

more poor bodies, with and without name – the dawn of a new day for those who remain,
those who cry, those who will not forget them. Never.

Non chiedetemi di fare la stessa fine e non posso mettere un lucchetto ai miei sentimenti, percorrere lo stesso sentiero così come non posso chiedere a due soli di splendere o morire assieme. E non posso vagare né a est né a ovest...

Do not ask me to face the same end, I cannot put a lock on my feelings, along the same path, as I cannot ask the sun at sunset to shine or die at the same time. And I can not wander either east or west ...

Dinnae speir at me ti reach the same end; I cannae sneck up my feelins, alang the same peth, like I cannae speir at twa suns ti shine or dee thegither. And I cannae stravaig either aist or wast ...

Hì hò edrè hi hò dun hi hiò edrè hi hiò dun
Hì ho edrè hò dun hio edrè hiò dun

The Disperate battle – risuona al campo,
lontano Barney Bree soffia struggente per
Eddie e Alec caduti all'alba.

Dobbiamo morire perché sappiamo,
morire col sorriso della gaia giovinezza,
morire con le mani che brillano di vita.

Ma la polvere soffia attorno, si
è fermata sopra le orecchie, loro per sempre
non più dormienti, ma morti.

Inutile negare le ossequiose falsità
della memoria, sono irrilevanti. C'è ben
poco per fermarli... sopravvissuti per caso.

In questa terra di morte noto una tomba isolata,
rimetto un pezzo di croce caduto. Mi
siedo accanto. Rimembranze.

Hi hò edrè hi hò dun hi hiò edrè hi hiò dun/ Hi hò edrè hò dun hio edrè hiò dun/ The Desperate
Battle – resounds in the field, Barney Bree blows away, yearning for Eddie and Alec who died at
dawn./ Because we know we must die, die with a smile of gay youth die with hands that glow
of life./ But the dust blowing around, Stops above the ears, for they were no longer asleep, but

Hì hò edrè hi hò dun hi hiò edrè hi hiò dun
Hì ho edrè hò dun hio edrè hiò dun

The Desperate Battle – stounds ti the field,
faur aff Barney Bree blaws awa, grienin fir
Eddie and Alec, deid at dawin.

Because we ken we maun dee
dee wi a smile o blythe youthheid,
dee wi haunds that leam wi life.

But the stour blawin aroun
stapped ower their lugs, fir they aye
were nae langer sleepers, but deid.

Yuiseless ti nae-say the sleekit lees
o memory: thon's aa buff. There's nae muckle
ti stap thaim ... survived, bi chaunce.

In this laund o daith I ken o a lane lair,
whaur I lay a piece o a cowpit cross.
I sit aside it. Remembraunce.

dead./ No denying that the obsequious falsities of memory are irrelevant. There is very little to
stop them ... survived by chance./ In this land of death, I know a a lonely tomb I lay down a piece
of the fallen cross. I sit beside it. Remembrance.

The Anzio Pipe Band May 1944: Hamish's pipe band performs for wounded American troops at Nettuno

© Felicity Henderson

(Anzio Pipe Band, Anzio 1944) - Hamish in centre with pipers from Gordons, Seaforth, and Royal Scottish Fusiliers battalions

© Felicity Henderson

*Non abbiate paura se qualcuno costruirà la vostra scena finale;
taglierà il cordone ombelicale come ultimo ed estremo atto: il
taglio finale. Una vita che si spezza per sempre. Come sta la
luna quando non si hanno le stelle e dove finiscono quando
non brillano più? Si formano in me incubi, cicatrici, sangue e
ferite passione e sogno luce e oscurità.*

Do not be afraid if someone will construct your final scene, cut the umbilical cord as the last and
final act: the final cut. A life that is broken forever. How does the moon fee; when there are no

Dinnae be feart gin a body shapes yer final scene: wha will cut the umbilical cord as the lest and awfy act: the final cut. A life that's brakken fir aye. Hou dis the müne feel whan there's nae starns and whaur dae they gang whan they nae langer shine? Nichtmares shape theirsels in me, scarts, stangs, smits and skaithed passioun and I dream licht and mirk.

stars and where do they go when they no longer shine? Nightmares take shape in me, scars, wounds, blemish and blood, passion and dream, light and darkness.

Una danza, per favore, una qualsiasi...
per ballare... voglio ballare – che sia delle
nostre parti: una danza per la vittoria.

I ragazzi sembrano più energici. Lungo il corso
di questa piccola città – anche i loro kilt
mostrano colori che adornano la notte.

Negli angoli più bui si è in attesa di sorprese,
le nostre forme alte sono ombre incorniciate
sui muri: introducono la notte dei ricordi.

"Via ora con questa danza – le nostre
dame possono andare all'inferno; rumori,
spari, urla: ecco il rincorrersi.

E' il fremito, l'agitarsi tale e quale al
gomito del violinista che per tutto il
tempo si muove, in questa notte.

Un abile sfregio, sanguinano le interiora della
tristezza – il vento comincia a rigare i volti, fatica,
paura: come indemoniati si urla per il lavoro.

"Che vadano all'inferno con i loro oboi e
le loro viole, i loro flauti e violoncelli,
e concertine! Fanculo!

Ora risuonano le nostre cornamuse, i nostri ottoni...
solo loro suppliscono ai più reconditi desideri
delle nostre piccole amanti.

"Dài Billy così come fa Danny,
martelleremo il vecchio Mussolini, seppelliremo
la nostra malinconia in compagnia".

A dance, a dance, please, any ... I want to dance ... a dance – from where we belong: a dance
for victory./ The boys seem more energetic. Along the corso of this small town – even their
kilts show colours that adorn the night./ In the darkest corners surprises await us, our forms
are shadows framed high on the walls: introduce the night of memories./ "Gone now with this
dance – our ladies can go to hell, noise, gunshots, screams, here is the chase./ And the thrill,

A daunce, a daunce, please, ony ...
I want a daunce ... a daunce frae
oor airt: a daunce fir victory.

The louns seem mair virrsome. Alang the corso
o this wee toun – even their kilts
shaw colours that decore the nicht.

I the daurkest neuks we byde fir surprises,
oor shapes are shaddaes framed heich
on the waas: bring in the nicht o memories.

'Thon's the wey wi this daunce – oor
leddies can gang ti hell: dirdum,
gunshots, yellochin: here's the chase.

And the dirl, the dinnle ti
the fiddler's elbuck that's in
constant motion, through the nicht.

A skeelie scaurin, bleedin frae the guts o
dool – the wind begins ti scart the faces, the darg,
dreid: like the damned cryin oot fir wark.

'Lat thaim gang ti hell wi their oboes and
their violas, flutes and cellies,
and concerteenies! Fuck thaim!

Nou oor pipes and bress stound ...
hit's thaim, juist, replace the inmaist desires
o oor young lovers.

'C'mon Billy, forby Danny,
we'll hammer auld Mussolini, we'll beerie
oor dowieness in guid fellaeship.'

the excited state to the fiddler's elbow that for all time moves on this night./ A skilled scarring,
bleeding from the interiors of sadness ¬– the wind begins to scratch the faces, hard work, pain,
possessed as you scream for work./ "Let them go to hell with their oboes and their violas, cellos
and their flutes, and concertinas! Fuck it!/ Now our bagpipes resonate, our brass ... only they are
a match for the innermost desires of our young lovers./ "Come on Billy , likewise Danny, we will
pound the old Mussolini, bury melancholy in our company."

*Che cosa posso ricordare, sognare, fermare nella mia testa.
Un momento, un attimo: lui con la sua bella divisa, orgoglio
dei suoi cari, fermo nel mezzo di una spiaggia. Lo guardo, gli
giro attorno e vedo un coltello piantato dietro la schiena.
Non c'è sangue. Stringo un mazzetto di papaveri nella mano e
guardo le onde del mare giungere al termine della loro corsa,
si fermano al capolinea e non fanno più ritorno.
All'inferno tutti i diavoli mentre cade l'angelo del fuoco.*

Fine

Pino Mereu, dicembre 2011

What can I remember, a dream, kept in my head. A moment, an instant: him with his beautiful uniform, pride of his family, standing still in the middle of a beach. I look at him, I walk round him and I see a knife in his back. There is no blood. I hold a bunch of poppies in my hand and

Whit can I mynd o, dreamin, hauden in my heid. A moment, a blink: him wi 's braw uniform, prood o his faimily, staunin aye in the mid o a beach. I look at him, I walk aroun him and see a knife in his back. There's nae bluid. I haud a bunch o poppies in my haund and watch the waves rax and feenish, they stap at the end and dinnae gang back.

Gang ti hell aa the deils while the angel o fire faas.

watch the waves run and finish, they stop at the end and don't go back.
Go to hell all the devils while the angel of fire falls.

Anzio Pipe Band at Fori Imperiali, Roma, 15 June 1944

© Felicity Henderson

A New Voice on the Carrying Stream

Fred Freeman

I speak to you, companions of revelry,
Drunk like me on words,
Sword-words, poison-words,
Key-words, lockpicker-words,
Salt-words, mask and nepenthe.
The place we're going to is silent
Or deaf. It's the limbo of the lonely and the deaf.
You'll have to run the last lap deaf,
You'll have to run the last lap by yourself.[1]

In many respects, Primo Levi is an apt starting point for our reflection on Hamish Henderson. It was Henderson who first translated Levi's poignant 'Shema' into English; both men repeatedly recounted how Auschwitz, racism and the H-bomb had changed the whole consciousness of the twentieth century and role of the artist in society; both, using different metaphors, would compare themselves to Coleridge's Ancient Mariner, surviving, as Henderson puts it so soberly in his 'First Elegy', only to 'bear witnesss'. How very like Primo Levi's rhetorical voice and tone in their entreaty to do something *now* – 'Before the leaves fall, Before the sky closes again'... – are Hamish Henderson's lines :

Now, now: before another silence
invades our eyes, before another wind rises
... before rust flowers again.[2]

---

[1] Primo Levi, 'Voices', *Shema: Collected Poems*, London: The Menard Press, 1976.

[2] Hamish Henderson, 'Colour of Rain and Iron', *Collected Poems and Songs*, edited by Raymond Ross, Edinburgh: Curly Snake Publishing, 2000, p.134.

Both poets were disturbed by the return of an idiot complacency and the renewed prospect of that 'familiar pounding of iron footsteps / In front of our doors';[3] 'Death... heard weeping' when 'In the heart of life's town / ... no watch we're keeping'.[4]

These were not the words of prophets of doom but of artists who recognised that man was caught up, to use Henderson's own expression, in 'a millennial conflict'; that, in view of this, art and the artist would bear a special responsibility 'to reconcile and heal' ('Sixth Elegy'), 'to speak truly / With a middle voice' ('To Hugh MacDiarmid'). But that would not prove an easy task. As George Steiner rightly claimed in his *Language And Silence*, and men like Levi and Henderson knew fine, the world of Auschwitz – and the twentieth-century experience – 'lies outside speech as it lies outside reason'. Where men were referred to as 'Stücke' (pieces), and 'Arbeit Macht Frei' (Work Makes One Free) literally meant, with cruel irony, that one would be worked to death or worked into a physical and mental state in preparation for the crematoria, a violence had been done to language. Mulling over what had happened to language in Europe, George Orwell would assert, in a searching essay of 1946, that political jargon, in particular, was now designed 'to make lies sound truthful and murder respectable.' Words had been corrupted of their meaning. Language had become impoverished, empty, futile.

How, then, to find a meaningful voice? Levi's answer was to explore mythology, metaphors, etymology, euphemisms, colloquial expressions. Henderson, too, would find his 'middle voice' in drawing upon mythology, colloquial speech, folk humour and, much like Burns, a Scots bilingualism; or, at times, a tortuously incongruous mix of linguistic registers. Take the short passage:

> Think, and think long
>   On all that horror, history's saturnalia:
> The tortuous power-webs,
>   the boxes, the alcoves,
> the souped-up ideologies,
>   the lying   memoranda,
> the body count,
>   the tenders for crematoria,

---

3 Primo Levi, 'Waiting', *Shema: Collected Poems*.

4 Hamish Henderson. 'Death', *Collected Poems and Songs*, p.31.

the wire, the ramp,
   the unspeakable experiments
White earth   not earth...

It is the sharp juxtaposition of colloquialisms – 'souped-up
ideologies' and 'power-webs' against the Latinisms like 'saturnalia',
conjuring-up the mirthful ancient Roman festival of Saturn and
sitting so uneasily with that other Latinate word, 'crematoria', that
underlines the whole hideously inhumane process: the mundanity
of keeping 'memoranda' (literally, informal records); 'the tenders
for crematoria' (i.e., the shabby minutiae of genocide); 'the wire'
strung by uncaring human hands. Moreover, the enumeration of
horrors, metrically paced like so many matter-of-fact things being
ticked off an inventory list, and ending in that awful image, 'White
earth   not earth', forces one to stop and think again. Nobody has
ever quite said this before with the same strange, eerie, unfamiliar
voice. The perception is alarming, alienating.

   Henderson, in fact, knew he was doing something quite
different. When asked, somewhat offhandedly in a 1978 interview,
whether he felt 'cut off from contemporary English poetry', he
boldly replied:

> Oh – I am cut off... I think I'm doing something different. I
> don't make any boundary between poetry and song. I write
> about the most pressing problems of all – namely those of
> our continuing existence... [5]

He was well aware of having both a different motivation and a
different *modus operandi* from that of most contemporary poets
anywhere in Britain. For him, the prevailing 'art for art's sake'
ethos was futile. A poet, worthy of the title, was to be an active
agent; a reshaper of his environment; a veritable 'makar'. Or, he
(she) was nothing.

   You, my poems, were not created
   To pander to gentle nostalgias,
   Poetic play-acting, languishing mummery.
   You, my poems, were not created

---

[5] Timothy Neat, *Hamish Henderson: A Biography, Vol.II: Poetry Becomes
People, 1952-2002*, Edinburgh: Birlinn, 2009, p.90.

To help humanity escape from the jaws
Of the famished wolves of their misery.
You, my poems, are my weapons![6]

He goes on to speak of 'those that call themselves pure poets': the
'impoverished ... solitary and blind...'
In this connection and, no doubt, with Gramsci at the back of
his mind, he would evolve quite original theories of art and poetry.
He would begin to differentiate between two types of art: art 'for
Art's sake', which 'is bad art, art gone rotten, and is hardly worth
the name at all...,'[7] and art (in this case, 'literature') which 'must
desire to be life not an idea of life...'[8] As he says so aptly in 1941:

> I am tired of reading poems which have an atmosphere of
> 'Here is Art'. I want poems with the atmosphere 'Here is
> Life', and this is Hamish Henderson living it.[9]

In one of his WEA lectures, entitled 'The Role of the Artist in
Society', he observes :

> Art depends on the society. In primitive societies the poet
> or bard was an honoured person. Integrally part of the
> community. His songs or hymns were part of reality for
> the people...(But) In all class societies the completeness
> of the artist's perception of reality is to a certain extent
> crippled...Gradually the poet and the community must be
> threaded together again – and we must start here, where
> we stand...[10]

In practical terms, what had all these exalted notions to do with
Hamish Henderson? Everything. Here was a serious scholar and
academic decrying academia; an established 'art' poet – recipient

---

[6] Hamish Henderson, 'My Poems', *Collected Poems and Songs*, p.104.

[7] Timothy Neat, *Hamish Henderson: A Biography, Vol.I: The Making of the Poet, 1919-1953*, Edinburgh: Birlinn, 2007, p.37.

[8] *Ibid*, p.189.

[9] *Ibid*, p.56.

[10] *Ibid*, pp.235-36.

of the Somerset Maugham Award for Poetry – castigating his
fellow art poets; a lone voice calling for a cultural revolution.

> The time has come for contemporary art-poets to renew
> their energies – not in debate in university seminar rooms,
> not in the pages of small magazines, but in direct contact
> with the folk poets. Intellectual enquiry is one thing, art
> something else.[11]

Fine. But how was that such a radical departure from so much that
had come before? Had not Burns, in his arguments with editor
George Thomson, insisted upon a more authentic 'native' folk
humour and expression? Had not Wordsworth, in his 'Prologue'
to The Lyrical Ballads, inveighed against the 'gaudiness and inane
phraseology' of 'modern writers' in calling for a new poetry,
drawing upon the 'plainer...more emphatic language' of humble
rustics? Yes. But these were still artists who under various guises –
whether they be that of 'ploughman poet' or what have you – did
not quite cross the critical divide between subject and object, art
and artifact.

Henderson, arguably more than any other 'art' poet in Britain
(and greatly to the detriment of his formal reputation), would
cross that divide from the very outset of his career. Amongst the
swaddies in North Africa and Italy, he was, according to General
Tam Wimberley, already a 'legend' by the early 1940s. Here was a
soldier in the field who penned popular songs – and collected so
many songs and ballads amongst allied soldiers and POWs alike –
that were to be sung in the camps and in the theatres of war. It
is thus his voice – a genuine swaddie's voice – and the collective
folk voice that we hear in his songs and poems throughout those
campaigns and, as we shall see, in so much of the material he
would write throughout his life.

Looking, for example, at 'The 51st Highland Division's Farewell to
Sicily', which he wrote (with 'the words flooding into my head') as
he witnessed the 153 Brigade of the Highland Division preparing the
troops for a return to Scotland, we find the multiple voice of the
artist in the field. There are two poetic voices here: a ballad voice
and a folk voice: one, aptly, distant and impersonal – what Willa
Muir has termed, in describing the ancient ballads, 'the underworld

---

[11] Ibid, p.285.

of feeling', devoid of 'emotional gurglings'; the other, minutely intimate and personal. Henderson effects this through employing a hauntingly ominous ballad frame and tone to relate quite directly the actual thought processes of the soldiers. The impersonal voice is that of the anonymous, ballad narrator – appropriately a tragic, prophetic voice against which the individual swaddie knows he has no control. It structurally occupies the opening, middle and closing lines of the song like disturbingly fixated thoughts that will not go away. And it is this anonymous Scots ballad voice that, ineluctably and tragically, foretells more bloodshed on the horizon. It is the voice of destiny, somewhat reminiscent of all the tragic ballads that have come before: very like the words of Gilgamesh, when he says – 'I must travel an unknown road and fight a strange battle'.

> The sky ow'r Messina is unco an' grey,
> (altered or strange)
> An aa the bricht chaulmers are eerie
> (bright stars, disturbingly ominous)
>
> Aa the bricht chaulmers are eerie[12]

But it is quite another narrator – a living participant, not at all anonymous, and speaking with the colloquial voice of battle weary men – who enunciates, almost conversationally, the whole mood of the regiment in one, simple reiterated reflection:

> Puir bliddy swaddies are wearie[13]
> (poor bloody soldiers)

It is he, this folk overseer and participant, who cinematically chronicles the entire scene at the end of the Sicilian campaign. It is he, as participant, who both describes the actions of the men in Scots – from the 'dozie' and 'fey' (other worldly) pipie who 'winna come roon the day' to the chappie who has 'beezed himself up for a photy' (spruced himself up); and it is he who enunciates so convincingly the voice of sad reflection and departure – the poignant

---

[12] Hamish Henderson, 'The 51st Highland Division's Farewell to Sicily', *Collected Poems and Songs*, pp.84-85.

[13] *Ibid*, p.84.

'farewell' that runs throughout the song. His is the collective voice of what every swaddie was thinking in bidding farewell to Sicily: namely, now let's bloody well get on with it... come what may. And it is conveyed subtly, as with the old classic ballads, via objects (pipes and drums) rather than through undiluted emotions.

> Then tune the pipes and drub the tenor drum
> (Leave your kit this side o the wa)
> Then tune your pipes and drub the tenor drum
> Aa the bricht chaulmers are eerie.

Again, in the 'Ninth Elegy', we are confronted with two poetic voices – two registers of speech – which embody our artist / participant. And they are neatly divided, in this short poem, into two sections corresponding to the poet as objective diarist / observer, in the opening, and projected self / soldier, in the remaining lines. This is effected through the neat mental projection which merges the mind of observer and participant into one shared consciousness and is so casually introduced with the line: 'His thought was like this'.

> For there will come a day
> *When the Lord will say*
> *– Close Order!*

> One evening, breaking a jeep journey at Capuzzo
> I noticed a soldier as he entered the cemetery
> and stood looking at the grave of a fallen enemy.
> Then I understood the meaning of the hard word 'pietas'
> (a word unfamiliar to the newsreel commentator
> as well as to the pimp, the informer and the traitor).

> His thought was like this.– Here's another 'Good Jerry'!
> Poor mucker. Just eighteen. Must be hard-up for man-
> power.
> Or else he volunteered, silly bastard. That's the fatal,
> The-fatal-mistake. Never volunteer for nothing.
> I wonder how he died? Just as well it was him, though,
> and not one of our chaps... Yes, the only good Jerry,
> as they say, is your sort, chum.

> Cheerio, you poor bastard.
> Don't be late on parade when the Lord calls 'Close Order'.
> Keep waiting for the angels. Keep listening for Reveille.[14]

This dual voice enables Henderson to make both a monumental statement and, equally, a very personal statement about war and death. Here at once is the high register of the diarist speaking with august formality of 'a fallen enemy'; of 'pietas', an ancient Roman word pregnant with meaning – piety, patriotism, familial affection but also, given the context, 'pieta', that haunting Christian image of Mary with the dead body of Christ. The idiom, so familiar in the Great War poets, is cold; remote, the images having been chisselled so many times in stone and word. To my mind, they conjure up those memorable lines :

> Dulce et Decorum est
> Pro patria mori.

> (It is sweet and right to die for your country)[15]

It has all been said before; so many times, in fact, that even the irony of the words (the fact being that you would have to be alive to appreciate the sentiment) has been sapped of its meaning. Henderson needs a different idiom, so he reverts to the language he would have used with his men over a pint in 'Alex' (Alexandria): the coarse colloquial of a pub or shebeen blether. How else could he project his thoughts so effectively into that of the lone soldier at the German's graveside? It is this strikingly 'defamiliarised' low register of language, coarse and ungrammatical, that will enable him – really his surrogate self – to give vent to his innermost feelings as he addresses the young German, with the mixture of pity and disdain that the common swaddie in the field would so obviously have felt: 'Poor mucker... silly bastard... Yes, the only good Jerry, as they say, is your sort, chum. Cheerio, you poor bastard.'

That Henderson knew he was exploring somewhat unploughed ground linguistically is clear from his central criticism of poets like W. R. Rodgers, whom he otherwise admired:

---

[14] Hamish Henderson, 'Ninth Elegy', *Collected Poems and Songs*, p.70.

[15] See Wilfred Owen 'Dulce et Decorum est', in *The Poems of Wilfred Owen*, London: Wordsworth Poetry Library, 1994, p.60.

> Sometimes Rodgers' diction is too strained... his literary
> language would do well to dip down to common Irish folk
> speech again for a lyrical impulse... this is an old melody for
> a new makar... [16]

It is even clearer from his praise of those like Yeats and Auden who
had 'experimented successfully with the folk idiom'; those like W.
S. Graham who had 'carried the experiments a stage further.'[17]
Moreover, Henderson was, in fact, advocating something wholly
different from the literary experimenters: a veritable return to the
oral tradition as he mixed and melled with swaddies and POWs;
eventually devoting so much of his time either leading a Scottish
Folk Revival from his unofficial headquarters at Sandy Bell's pub –
'talking to little poets', as one Scots academic put it so cavalierly, or
in living himself in Travellers' camps. He knew where his priorities
lay:

> My commitment was to the oral tradition. The choices were
> – success at my desk or failure in the berry-fields. I chose
> the dreels (life energy) o' Blairgowrie – and life with the
> Stewarts.[18]

True; but not quite an accurate statement. Was this not the same
man who had penned 'Rivonia' – sung by the freedom fighters
in the fields of South Africa and personally recognised by Nelson
Mandela? Or 'The Freedom Come-All-Ye', acknowledged by
Pete Seeger, Bob Dylan, and the whole Irish and Scottish folk
movements as being one of the best and most far reaching songs
of the century? I think there was, unquestionably, still an active
hand at that desk.

But he was, indeed, 'cut-off from contemporary English poetry';
he had, as I say, crossed a divide between artist and subject that
serious elegists and poets simply did not cross. Furthermore, he
alone – long before the likes of Bob Dylan – did 'not make any
boundary between poetry and song' when, even more so than at
the time of Burns, the 'lesser lyric' (song) had no literary status
whatsoever. In a significant letter of 1949, E. P. Thompson would

---

[16] Timothy Neat, *Hamish Henderson*, Vol.I, p.73.

[17] Timothy Neat, *Hamish Henderson*, Vol.II, p.139.

[18] *Ibid*, p.44.

commend him for being 'more than any other poet I know...
an instrument through which thousands of others can become
articulate' and would stress the importance of his song and ballad
writing – 'quite as important as the Elegies'.[19]

On the other hand, most of the English poets loathed what he was
doing. So did contemporary Scottish poets like Hugh MacDiarmid,
who would maintain in an ongoing *Scotsman* newspaper debate:

> The demand everywhere today is for higher and higher
> intellectual levels. Why should we be concerned then with
> songs which reflect the educational limitations, the narrow
> lives, the poor literary abilities, of a peasantry we have
> happily outgrown?[20]

Henderson, though out on a cultural limb, was, nonetheless, clear
and uncompromising in his support of the oral tradition:

> It is only the diminutives among the art poets who openly
> attack and despise oral folk culture, usually for vulgar
> reasons of exclusiveness and precocity – but the top-
> notchers sense the stimulus that the ballads and vernacular
> austerity can give.[21]

And it was not just language that he had in mind. Behind it all were
serious philosophical notions about the 'folk'. In his essay, 'It Was
In You That It A' Began', he quotes Gramsci to the effect that

> 'folksong... is a separate and distinct way of perceiving life
> and the world, as opposed to that of "official" society.'[22]

In many respects it enabled him to find that elusive 'middle voice'
he had always sought and, to my mind, this was one of his most

---

[19] Hamish Henderson, *The Armstrong Nose: Selected Letters of Hamish Henderson*, edited by Alec Finlay, Edinburgh: Polygon, 1996, p.29.

[20] *Ibid*, p.119.

[21] Timothy Neat, *Hamish Henderson*, Vol.II, p.139.

[22] in Edward J Cowan (ed.), *The People's Past: Scottish Folk – Scottish History*, Edinburgh: Polygon, 1980, pp.4-16, p.14. The quotation is from Gramsci's *Letteratura e Vita Nazionale*, 1947-51.

critical discoveries. Almost in passing, and stated as succinctly as one can possibly imagine, he notes, in one of his many outlines, the Travellers'

> ...concrete awareness of the dualities of existence...[23]

This was, in fact, what he admired most in the culture of the Travellers, and it was manifestly what he shared with earlier Scottish writers who had also written in the wake of social upheavals: the Reformation, Scottish Civil Wars, Jacobite Rebellions, Agrarian Revolutions, Highland Clearances, the Great War. There is not sufficient time to discuss the whole phenomenon of the dual vision in Scottish literature: from Henryson's sheep that drolly challenges God on the subject of justice ('The Taill of the Scheip and the Doig'); Fergusson's 'Undecent' city of 'stews' and 'bawds', shite and 'Death' which, through the whole rational of *concordia discors* – a harmonic balance of opposites – is transmuted into an Auld Reikie that 'Lifts the soul from earth to sky' ('Auld Reikie'); Hogg's 'Witch of Fife'; Scott's *Waverley* with its balanced historical perspective – the dialectical weighing-up of pros and cons of the Jacobite cause – that so appealed to Avrom Fleischman and George Lukacs. But this too was part of a collective consciousness and is part of a carrying stream of its own.

An oral tradition and a unique literary tradition. That is exactly what he advocated: folk poetry and art poetry in direct contact, and both reflecting 'the dualities of existence'. So, a duality indeed. His poems are imbued with what he calls an 'incarnate dialectic' ('Heroic Song for the Runners of Cyrene'); 'the twin dragons, Life and Death, / Jousting thegither' ('Under the Earth I Go'); 'oppressed oppressors' ('Interlude'); 'saints and drunkards / ...madmen and angels' ('Written at a Conference'). But how did he actually achieve such a dual voice? Well, an insanely demonic humour was one of his means. In an appreciation of Picasso, Henderson acutely opines that

> Picasso's fauns and centaurs have the same artistic function as Shakespeare's clowns. In both, 'the ancient wisdom,

---

[23] Timothy Neat, *Hamish Henderson*, Vol.II, p.51.

disguised as laughter, dances with the light of a great summer sea'.[24]

Consider his uneasy perceptions in the heat of the desert war. Alongside the agonised portrayal of 'suffering and death' ('Heroic Song...'), and his slightly later references to 'the blood of my song',[25] is the outrageously Swiftean reduction of El Alamein to a personal battle with 'a raging toothache' and the ultimate salvation of a damaged tooth – the 'field dentist' operating on victims 'straight out of Hieronymus Bosch' and insisting on preserving one of the poet's molars ('Byspale in Benghazi'). Henderson would develop this mad folk humour and art as a civilising force to offset the enormities of war: his own inimitable way of jamming the death machine.

Beyond that, it was a means of setting his ideas into relief with a new, fresh voice: what the Russian formalists called 'defamiliarisation'. Take, for example, one of his most finely distilled poems, written on departure from the 'African deadland'.

So Long[26]

To the war in Africa that's over – goodnight.

To thousands of assorted vehicles, in every stage of
    decomposition
    littering the desert from here to Tunis – goodnight.

To thousands of guns and armoured fighting vehicles
    brewed up, blackened and charred
    from Alamein to here, from here to Tunis – goodnight.

To thousands of crosses of every shape and pattern,
    alone or in little huddles, under which the
        unlucky bastards lie –
            goodnight.

---

[24] Letter to the *Daily Worker*, quoted in Timothy Neat, *Hamish Henderson*, Vol.I, pp.266-67.

[25] Timothy Neat, *Hamish Henderson*, vol.I, p.175.

[26] Hamish Henderson, *Collected Poems and Songs*, p.77.

Horse-shoe curve of the bay
    clean razor-edge of the escarpment
tonight it's only the sunset that's blooding you.

Halfaya and Sollum: I think that at long last
    we can promise you a little quiet.
So long. I hope I won't be seeing you.

To the sodding desert – you know what you
    can do with yourself.

To the African deadland – God help you –
    and goodnight.

In the long tradition of poems like Fergusson's 'To the Tron-Kirk Bell', the whole monologue is based upon a conversation with the inanimate which neatly reduces all incongruities to one plane of perception (what, in the 'Third Elegy', he has deftly foreshadowed in his oxymoronic phrase: 'So long then, holy filth of the living'). And it is achieved as effortlessly as Fergusson through its loose colloquial language and its rhetorical structure. Note the deft use of anaphora (rhetorical repetition) which places the detritus of war (decomposed 'vehicles… littering the desert', burnt-out 'guns and armoured fighting vehicles') and the carnage of battle (thousands of crosses of every shape and pattern') on an equal footing: all part of the same informal leave taking.

To thousands of assorted vehicles...
To thousands of guns and armoured fighting vehicles...
To thousands of crosses of every shape and pattern...

The poetic voice is much like that of the swaddie at the young German's graveside in the 'Ninth Elegy'; it is the language of shebeen and bothy and the soldier's camp. But there is an added ingredient here: a light, at times crude, conversational tone and a relentless wit and humour; yes, conveyed as a wee, cheeky riposte at the end of five of the seven verses – 'goodnight' to 'war', to 'vehicles', to 'unlucky bastards', to the 'African deadland' – but so supremely understated in the line

> So long. I hope I won't be seeing you

and so daftly stated in *coorse* lines that would have made every swaddie chuckle:

> To the sodding desert – you know what you can do with yourself.

It is the daftness, the humour that makes it all bearable; it enables the soldier to confront the entire incongruous mess of men and machines, ambiguities and mixed emotions that he finds before him: all that is beyond simple explanation or rational analysis. Humour is for the poet, in the last analysis, the only means of reconciling the infernal and the mundane, the crudely physical and the spiritual, the serious and the bathetic. Ultimately, life and death. Tim Neat's remarks on the extended dialogue between Gershon Legman and Hamish Henderson on the subject of humour are germane here:

> The two men agreed that it was no coincidence that the Scots and the Jews have produced so many of the world's best comedians, and jokes. Both peoples share highly literate oral traditions; both use humour as a tool with which the confusions provoked – by migration, alienation, poverty, great wealth and murder – are addressed and come to terms with.[27]

As Legman himself put it in his introduction to *The Rationale of the Dirty Joke*: 'Tell me what you laugh at, and I will tell you what you are...'[28] How apt. The swaddie who bids his final 'So long...to the sodding desert' knows exactly who he is: a survivor...at least for the time being.

Closely related to his use of humour is Henderson's use of the bawdy. From the outset of the elegies he says of the dead: 'Their deaths were like their lives, human and animal'.[29] And it is

[27] Timothy Neat, *Hamish Henderson*, Vol.II, p.71.

[28] Gershon Legman, *The Rationale of the Dirty Joke*, New York: Basic Books/Grove Press, 1968.

[29] Hamish Henderson, 'First Elegy', *Collected Poems and Songs*, p.52.

that image, 'human and animal', which reminds me that both he and Burns used the bawdy with serious intent. Burns, essentially, said that man was an animal that urinated, defecated, copulated, lactated and so on, but who also aspired to the high spirituality of angels. Moreover, no reconciliation of such an inbuilt division could ever be achieved without a just appreciation of his dual nature: hence, his stinging satires on the Holy Willies of creation. As Henderson has it in one of his jottings,

> All the brutal facts of life need to be announced at once – we are all born, we copulate, we die. Consequently we are all entitled to an exaggerated plethora of sexual joy.[30]

Much like Burns, he assiduously collected and sang bawdry throughout his life, believing that within this side of the folk tradition resided a greater honesty about the human condition. As he affirms in his notes on folksong: 'It embraces the bawdy and stands for "human truth against the mummy-wrappings of sexual convention"'.

The bawdy gives rise (so to speak) to a surrealistic metaphorical turn in Henderson which we see peppered through his battlefield notebooks. At Alamein, for example, just hours after Rommel's attack on the southern flank, he describes

> Mark IIIs in various stages of dilapidation and an 88 looking like a petrified erection.[31]

Moreover, the bawdy is, in certain respects, Henderson's ultimate folk voice. It links him with the whole corpus of folk literature and folk humour which, as Legman observes, served both the Scots and the Jews for centuries as an outlet for their anger and frustration – a vent for centuries of deprivation and suffering. Wholly in keeping with this mixed perspective he would write in song – and dance with the Sixth Gordons in Italy – something of a 'comedy' (in Dante's sense of the word): 'Eightsome Reel'. A breathless reel, by its very nature an umremitting tension and a circular affair, this one

---

[30] Timothy Neat, *Hamish Henderson*, Vol.II, p.78.

[31] Timothy Neat, *Hamish Henderson*, Vol.I, p.84.

revolves round a dance of life / death, sex / blood and guts. It is a
potent mix of the swaddies' high libido –

> ferlies birling in the coaxing corners
> (essentially, having frantic sex in the corner)
> the randy reel-rawl (advancing) tae the rear
> (rawl is a ring of folk)
> 'pipes... (supplying) a' the needs of oor dear wee silly
> signorinas

and 'Thae bluid-reid billyboys' (Those blood-red mates') lurid
butchery in battle –

> Slash o' a dirk
> bleeds the guts o' the mirk   (out of the
> darkness)
> wi the glinting crammasies, the greens and yellows
>   (dark red blood)

And all resolving triumphantly in victory over 'Kesselring'; whom
'we'll ding doon... tae dee in the dyke-side' (defeat to die in a
ditch); old Musso', whom 'we'll pound... tae a weel-tanned tyke's
hide' (dog's hide).

The bawdy here, in this reel of sex, war and drink, which would
not be at all out of place in the dance of witches in 'Tam O' Shanter',
is really a Scots folk celebration, complete with 'poltergeists',
'tyke(s)', the deil's instrument – the pipes, the wildly wanton 'Auld
Hornie' himself (not the Christian devil at all, but a figure of orgies
and revelry) and, of course, that essential 'roun o drinks' that caps
any Scots celebration, folk or otherwise, from Hogmanay to the
celebration of birth and death.

> Ye mean
>   *crood o tinks*   (crowd of tinkers)
>   *gie's a fresh*
>   *roun o drinks*
> *An' we'll reel Auld Hornie and his gang tae glory.*[32]
>   (The Devil)

---

[32] Hamish Henderson, 'Eightsome Reel', *Collected Poems and Songs*, p.93.

Comic relief; the *couthie* folk voice of the swaddies letting their hair down; a just representation of humanity in the act, 'human and animal'. It says it all.

What is also important – and constitutes one of the greatest contributions to modern literature in Scots – is Henderson's understanding of the fluidity of folk language, the 'multi-ethnic origins of Scottish folk culture', the 'strength' residing in the hybridised nature of the tradition.'[33] And here he stands, almost a lone voice in the twentieth century, against the various Scots Society language purists, with their self-conscious double-thinking artificiality – whereby every word that remotely resembles English is to be expunged; MacDiarmid, with his 'Back to Dunbar' elitism – in which the high register of Scots (and *Jamieson's Dictionary*) are to be accorded pride of place; or even the nay-sayers like Muir, with his constrictive ideas of literature and language that, by definition, would have prevented someone like Issac Bashevis Singer from being properly recognised, let alone winning the Nobel Prize for his writings in Yiddish, the *patois* of the *shtetl*. Muir demanded that:

> The prerequisite of an autonomous literature is a homogeneous language. If Shakespeare had written in the dialect of Warwickshire, Spenser in Cockney, Ralegh in the broad Western speech which he used... English literature... would have lacked a common language where all the thoughts and feelings of the English people could come together, and serve as a standard for one another.[34]

Henderson would turn all these suppositions on their head. He was fond of quoting Stanley Hyman's 'masterly essay' of 1954:

> The finest Scottish poetry has always been bilingual in a curious fashion. Douglas the translator, Dunbar using Latin refrains, Boyd writing in Scottish and Latin, Burns writing in Scottish and English, are all poets for whom Lowland Scots

---

[33] Hamish Henderson, 'The Ballad and Popular Tradition to 1660', in *Alias MacAlias: Writings on Songs, Folk and Literature*, edited by Alec Finlay, Edinburgh: Polygon, 2004, pp.78-94.

[34] Edwin Muir, *Scott and Scotland*, Edinburgh: Polygon, 1982, p.4.

was one of the world's tongues, not the language in which God and Adam held converse.[35]

He thus had a clear idea that that there was no fundamental artistic or cultural problem with an unhomogeneous Scots language in either the oral tradition or, indeed, in an 'art' literature which had been 'cross-fertilised' (to use his exact expression) by that tradition.[36] In essence, he all but asserts, somewhat as *pawky* devil's advocate, that English is – and has long been – virtually a dialect of Scots. He refers to

> a resourceful creative togetherness: a sort of chemical fusion of two distinct but related ballad languages. In the folk field, as well as in the less agile literary Lallans, Scots may be said to include English and go beyond it.[37]

A *couthie* Scots folk voice, yes indeed; but, with Henderson you get the whole package. We may recall that his personal brief was to bring 'folk poets' and 'art-poets' together. Retracing his footsteps, literarily speaking, is not therefore an easy job. Take, for example, his 'Floret Silva Undique' (The Wood Is Flowering). To a degree, the poem is a restatement of the message of the 'Eightsome Reel' and so many of his other poems and songs: namely, 'the twin Dragons, Life and Death Jousting thegither' ('Under the Earth I Go'). But this is quite a sophisticated piece of artistry, full of so many meaningful allusions that it would take several pages of A4 to expound. The macaronic itself, with its 'Floret silva undique' refrain, harks back to another more famous ribald macaronic of the eleventh to twelfth centuries – 'Floret Silva Nobilis' (from *Carmina Burana*), the second verse of which reads:

> Floret silva undique.
> Nach mime gesellen ist mir we.
> ... Owi, wer sol mich minnen?

---

[35] Quoted in Hamish Henderson, '"At the Foot o' yon Excellin' Brae": The Language of Scots Folk-Song', *Alias MacAlias*, pp.51-77; p.52.

[36] Hamish Henderson, 'The Ballad, The Folk And The Oral Tradition', in Edward J Cowan (ed.), *Past and Present*, pp.69-107.

[37] Hamish Henderson, '"At the Foot o' yon Excellin' Brae"', p.53.

The wood is flowering all about
I grieve for my companion
...Alas who will love me?

This provides a perfect frame for what, in part, is something of a Burnsian 'Holy Fair' – 'a Sabbath stroll' with 'The rockin' righteous makin' hay': that is, a religious conventicle that amounts to an outdoor orgy in the Edinburgh meadows, full to capacity with 'Knox the poxy', 'Major Weir', 'Auld Nick's (the Devil's) wing ow'r a parish Kirk', 'Susanna's elders ...on the spree'. As with Burns, sanctimony is never far behind: 'The flesh is bruckle, the fiend is slee... (frail, devil is cunning) – a direct quote from Dunbar. In this respect, the poem may be seen to be an elaborate reply to Dunbar's poem with its dour refrain: 'Timor mortis conturbut me' (The fear of death distresses me): very much the opposite theme of 'Floret silva undique'.

> Oor pleasance heir is all vane glory,
> The fals warld is bot transitory,
> The flesche is brukle, the Fiend is sle :
> *Timor mortis conturbut me.*[38]

But that is only part of the equation. Our macaronic refrain that began 'Floret silva undique' goes on to read: 'The lily, the rose, the rose I lay'. And towards the middle of the poem we have 'The bailie beareth the bell away.' Both these lines are from an Elizabethan song of sexual contemplation regarding a hesitant virgin's concerns over her deflowering and the triumph of the bailie who obviously is about to put her through her paces.

> When I was in my mother's bower
> I had all that I would
>
> The bailey beareth the bell away
> The lily, the rose, the rose I lay
>
> ...

---

[38] William Dunbar, 'Lament for the Makars', *The Poems of William Dunbar*, edited by James Kinsley, University of Exeter Press, 1998.

And thro the glass window shines the sun.
How should I love and I so young?

The bailey beareth the bell away
The lily, the rose, the rose I lay.[39]

Furthermore, this song was said to have been sung during Durham's St George's festival in 'lusty May' and with festive guising – both of which are highlighted in the poem. Scots song and balladry are also part of the literary mix. There is the bawdry of Burns, never too far from the surface, as, with its suggestive rhythms, a Burnsian refrain propels forward the main activity of the day: 'Twa gaed tae the woods, and three cam hame'[40]:

> Spreid your thies, lass, and gie me room
> Twa gaed tae the woods, and three cam hame
> Reekie, tell me my true love's name
>
> Spread your thighs, lass, and give me room
> Two went to the woods, and three came home
> Edinburgh, tell me my true love's name [41]

And the line – 'To the greenwood must I go' – pawkily suggests a rewrite of the ballad 'Jock O' Braidislee', whereby 'Johnny' is to be spared by 'Balaam's ass', the good donkey of the Old Testament.

> To the greenwood must I go alas
> Could you gie me a loan o' Balaam's ass?

Everywhere, then, on this rampant May day in Reekie, is the triumph of sex and the life force over Calvinist gloom, doom and death. The following passage is exemplary :

---

[39] Anonymous, 'The Bridal Morn', in Sir Arthur Quiller-Couch (ed.), *The Oxford Book of English Verse, 1250-1918*, Oxford University Press, 1963, p.42.

[40] Robert Burns, 'The Bob o' Dumblane', in Andrew Noble and Patrick Scott Hogg (eds), *The Canongate Burns: The Complete Poems and Songs of Robert Burns*, Edinburgh: Canongate Classics, 2001, p.875.

[41] Hamish Henderson, 'Floret Silva Undique', *Collected Poems and Songs*, p. 142;

Floret silva undique
Sweet on the air till dark of day.
Sma' back pipes and they dance a spring.   (lively dance)
Over the grave all creatures sing.
The sun gangs doon under yon hill   (goes down)
Jenny and Jake are at it still.
To the greenwood must I go alas
Could you gie me a loan o' Balaam's ass?
Alano I dig you the most:
The lily I laid, the rose I lost.
Whit dae ye hear amang the broom? (within the fields of broom)
Spreid your thies, lass, and gie me room.
Twa gaed tae the woods, and three cam hame
Reekie, tell me my true love's name.
Edinburgh castle, toun and tour   (town and tower)
The gowans gay and the gilliefloor.   (daisies, carnation)
Luvers daffin' aneath the slae   (frolicking, blackthorn bush)
Floret silva undique
The bonniest pair ye iver seen
Fuckin' aneath the floor'in gean.   (blooming cherries)
Bairnies wankin' abuin the clay
Floret silva undique.[42]

Henderson thus uses multiple literary voices, and a very unhomogeneous variety of languages and literary registers, to present a Fergussonian vision of 'Reekie' (Edinburgh) which reconciles all its disparate elements – 'Davie Bowie' and 'Hornie', 'Knox' and 'Mac the Knife', 'Major Weir' and 'Deacon Brodie', 'Kimmers o' Coogate' (Gossips of the Cowgate) and 'elders… on the spree', 'Jenny and Jake' (the common folk) – through the socially levelling exercise of unadulterated sex. Linguistically, he has given us a hybrid pretty well beyond anything we have ever seen: Latin; a touch of French ('Edina-Reekie-mon amour'); various registers of English – Elizabethan, modern poetic English ('Sweet on the air till dark of day'), post 1960s English slang ('Tim and Eck from their pad in Sciennes – Cowboy T-shirts and Brutus jeans'); Scots – Dunbar's high register, Traveller's Cant ('The kinchin's bara' – the child is willing), Modern Metropolitan Scots ('Scrunchin hurdies and raw-bone heid / Junkies mell wi' the livin deid' (Tight

---

[42] Hamish Henderson, 'Floret Silva Undique', *Collected Poems and Songs*, p.142.

arses and *fig.* erections / Junkies mix with the living dead); snippets of Burns, Fergusson and the ballads, and, of course, pure bawdry of the highest order ('The bonniest pair ye iver seen / Fuckin' aneath the floo'r'in gean').

Something of a *tour de force*. And, perhaps, just the right note on which to leave any discussion of Hamish Henderson.

Occupied Space
A Look at Modern Scottish Poetry[1]

George Gunn

When the winner of the 2012 T.S. Eliot prize for poetry was announced in January, the event grabbed the attention of the media because two of those poets short-listed withdrew their books from the running when it was revealed that a financial investment company, Aurum, with a portfolio of hedge-funds, was sponsoring the competition. In the fallout from the 2008 'credit crunch' this, in the scheme of things, was a minor burn – but not without irony. If the Poetry Book Society, who organised the event, loose their Arts Council of England funding they are entitled to search for an alternative source of lucre even though the City of London may not be the most ethical place to acquire it. On the other hand, that is where all the cash of UK plc has gone, so 'a terrible symmetry is born,' if I could be forgiven for re-interpreting W.B. Yeats' famous phrase.

'Hedge-funds are at the very pointy end of capitalism,' said John Kinsella, one of the poets who withdrew his work in protest. Alice Oswald, the original objector, said that 'Poetry should be questioning not endorsing such institutions.' John Burnside, the prize winner, so articulate on the page, understandably proved less so under the forensic gaze of the TV cameras when he was asked what he thought about the 'protests'. Are Kinsella and Oswald genuine disaffected voices or are they ironical and inverse hecklers, whom the poet Tony Harrison has termed 'the rhubarbarians': instead of crying out against the mystification of poetry and art in general by the ruling class, as Harrison would have it, they instead complain that it is sullying its robes by associating with 'such institutions'?

---

[1] An earlier version of this piece was published under the title 'The art form of the Scottish heart' in *Scottish Review*, No. 534, 3 April 2012. Dedicated to Hamish Henderson, as he is the inspiration for most of what I think about poetry, song and culture.

As someone who has wrestled on the killing floor of conscience when a play he wrote was given an award which was to be presented by Prince Charles, my sympathies lie with both the refuseniks and the recipient. This is, as both John Burnside and I will attest, an impossible situation. But society and life within it generally presents itself in political terms and, as we do not inhabit Plato's republic of perfect forms – in contrast to my imperfect republican conscience – but rather plummet and ascend in the imbalances of society itself therefore, the argument runs, poetry, like everything else, has a function.

So what is it and what are poets for? The question hangs in the air of human achievement like so much smoke. The fire of the answer is obviously: to write poetry. But to accept that singularity would be to avoid the reality of human experience which constantly validates Louis MacNeice's awkward observation on 'the drunkenness of things being various.' Are poets right to question the shape of our society, or is their purpose purely to imagine its possibility in relation to themselves?

If poetry is on trial, then it may seem perverse to start off by putting forward the case for the prosecution; and if the charge is, are poets good for anything, then one answer would be: no, they are not. So what is the evidence?

To the casual observer it would appear that most contemporary poets – those who are put up for and win prizes, for these are the only ones they will hear about – are published in London and either work for publishers or teach 'creative writing' at a university. When their books appear, they are praised by a select few fellow travellers in journals read by an elevated band of their peers, supplicants or aspirants. On first reading, the poems produced by this group seem to be written in a secret language of Cabbalistic patterns and Masonic signs and signatures. This codification, as the distribution of literary prizes indicates, serves them well, as it occupies space, traditionally the open domain of the public mind, and is easily recognised by others with a similar training. They move about this occupied space, these poets, like agents at a conspiracy. They transmit their information to each other on a refined wavelength in messages constructed out of baroque scaffolding and arabesque surfaces where sentences swim through the sea of clutter, interference and desperation most people understand as reality, like a blind and deaf fish, much like the one recently discovered at the bottom of the sea.

The masters of indifference who manage this secret agency – in which each member is an active administrator – invite the public to swoon at the beauty of these messages and to praise the felicity of their construction and to reward the poet-messengers appropriately. The media fascination with literary awards has corresponded to the rarification of poetry itself. So it is that the 'new renaissance' (whisper it, 'the real renaissance') of poetry in Scotland has come to be. Note here that it is 'poetry in Scotland' not 'Scottish poetry' because it is one of the popular orthodoxies that 'national' definitions in regard to poetic output are contradictory, unhelpful, narrow and reactionary. This, of course, pre-supposes that 'poetry' comes out of no-where other than a singular human consciousness un-sullied by being born and brought up in Brechin as opposed to Belgravia. To those who subscribe to this phenomenon and who have displayed a keen facility in the secret language and who give great weight to the patterns and signs go the prizes which guarantee the poet entry into the small Dionysian where the Sun always rises in the eternal Springtime in the best of all possible fraternities.

In 1817 John Keats wrote a letter to his brothers George and Thomas in which he spoke of a 'negative capability'[2] and by this he meant to define his poetry as a defence of beauty against reason which he saw as the force driving Coleridge to objectify everything in terms of knowledge. Keats chose to make the claim for the liberty of the individual in order for them to define themselves in relation to systems as opposed to becoming a systems fodder. This has to be distinguished from the destructive individualism of the libertine right which allows for everything for everyone but which actually guarantees nothing for the majority. For Keats the world was beautiful because it contained 'uncertainties, mysteries, doubts' and, for all that the term 'romantic' has attached itself to his life and work, Keats was a man who studied the emerging scientific marvels of his time such as medicine and electricity and understood the negative pole of an electric current which is passive and receptive.

The 'current' one can detect in the poetry of 'the best of all possible fraternities,' when one deciphers the inverted runes and anti-oghams, is of a charge not there, of a space emptied as opposed to being filled. That the 'space between the words,' which is the maxim of the poetry workshop leader, is in fact just

---

[2] Ou Li, *Keats and Negative Capability*, London: Continuum, 2009, p. ix.

space and, unlike an atom, has no nucleus or electrons and as a result embraces neither the beauty Keats championed nor the knowledge Coleridge sought. If a writer rejects 'history' and 'subject' as being dogma then all that is really left is style, which is the 'space' between substance and meaning. A poetics based on this offers nothing and challenges nothing but fulfils the nervous ambivalence of the contemporary age which is resistant to commitment or meaning.

What Keats gave us when he ruminated on 'negative capability' was an articulation of the necessary questioning of everything, of accepting no system as being complete. In this regard he carried the mantle of Socrates. On the day of his death it is said that Socrates approached his disciples and those who would eventually kill him and told them he was 'setting' Aesop's Fables into verse. This flies in the face of the accepted Aristotelian credo that Socrates was illiterate. To compound this heresy, Socrates told those foregathered that he had had a dream. It was the usual recurring dream in which a voice ('the' voice) kept telling him to 'keep practicing the art'. Socrates had always taken this to mean the 'art' of philosophy but now, on the eve of his death, he realised that it was the 'art of writing' he should have engaged with. Sometimes enlightenment, even to the father of philosophy, comes too late. For Socrates this was ironically 'ironic' as his method in philosophy, as it was the in the art of the poetry of Keats, was one of constant questioning.

If that is the case for the prosecution, then I admit it is a poor thing, and if it appears that I deliberately undermine the evidence then I should remind you, as Wilde reminds us in 'The Ballad of Reading Goal', 'that each man kills the thing he loves'.[3] But what I am engaged in here is the pursuit of an answer to a question: what are poets for? There should be no need for a bitter look, a flattering word, a kiss or a sword. So to 'the' answer, to any case for the defence: it is that there must be a counter argument against the 'inverted runes and anti-oghams' of those who fortify the occupied space of poetry's once open domain; 'questioning' as opposed to 'endorsing'.

Writing poetry in Scotland has never been, despite the establishment of the myth to the contrary, a singular and obscure monastic discipline for a chosen elite, or an isolated or marginalised

---

[3] Oscar Wilde, *The Ballad of Reading Gaol and Other Poems*, London: Penguin Classics, 2010, p.4.

activity undertaken by sallow cheeked youths 'half in love with easeful death,' to reference John Keats yet again.[4]

Anglo-centric literary orthodoxy places the poet at the edge of society, engaged in the production of an art which only a few well educated individuals with the necessary time and resources can understand. The majority of people, or 'the lave' as they are called in Aberdeenshire, are excluded from this hierarchy in much the same way as an ordinary person is denied entrance into a convention of safe crackers: they simply do not know the code.

Education, in general, encourages the individual to aspire to reach up and appreciate what the playwright John McGrath called 'the cultural jewels on the top shelf': to crack the code and join the club.[5] The emphasis here is on rising up, of leaving what you know behind, of rejecting your own culture as somehow inferior. McGrath's entire creative life was spent reacting against his educational background and was a sustained attack on the 'top shelf' in order to bring the 'cultural jewels' crashing down onto the scullery floor so that 'the lave' can give them a good kicking about to see just what they are made of. As is usual when the structures of dominance, which cultural exclusion rests upon, are examined they are found to be no more than the shadow-puppets in Plato's cave: an illusion. Once the sham is exposed then culture can be seen for what it is: the result of people living together in society. Art is the expression of that. Poetry is a craft within that art.

The poetic evolution of Scotland reveals a different narrative, offers us a more optimistic and inclusive literary tradition full of 'cultural jewels' of a more egalitarian nature. From my position within my 'open domain', which is Caithness and Sutherland, the view of both where poetry has come from and where it is going takes on a different perspective – literally, like looking through the other end of the telescope – from that of Anglo-centric orthodoxy. In the north Highlands we have a duality of poetic traditions: that of the Celtic 'bard' and of the Norse 'skald'. I place them both between inverted commas to differentiate between them and the appellation of 'poet'. Time and cultural erosion have melded and reduced the function of bard and the skald into that of the poet but the popular conception and practice of the contemporary poet

---

[4] John Keats, 'Ode to a Nightingale' , in *The Complete* Poems, London: Penguin Classics, 2nd ed., 1977, p.347.

[5] John McGrath, *A Good Night Out*, London: Nick Hern Books, 1996.

denies the residual influence of the bard and the skald onto what poetry was, is and could become. This denial contributes to the loss of a collective cultural memory and consolidates poetry's current position as that of an, at best, worthy irrelevance or something rolled out, when it is needed, as some kind of totemistic grotesque at such events as Burns Suppers, weddings or funerals.

Far from being at the edge of society or in the periphery of significance, both the bard and the skald were at the centre of their respective cultures' 'society'; which is again put between inverted commas here, too, as an indication that 'society' is a consequence of 'culture', not the other way around. Both bards and skalds were given great status in pre-Norman Scotland because they were storehouses of the people's stories, their dreams and creation myths.

The Norse looked to the skald and the Celts looked to the bard for an articulation of both their secular psychology, their ways of being and social interaction and for an explanation as to why the sky would not fall on them. The bard and the skald gave valediction and expression to the cult of the ancestors and mapped out a pathway into the future. They may have woven their alphabet from trees or cut their messages in runes onto flagstone but their social and cultural function was defined and necessary and available to all, for the story they told was the story of the tribe, and the light they shone on that collective was the light of life.

Poetry, for the Celts and the Norse, was the music of their blood. It was the medium through which they understood themselves. Despite the attempts of the various hierarchies who have organised society in order that they rule over it, poetry is that medium still. Which is why, despite its obscure codifications and institutionalised elitism, its canonisation and cultural misuse, poetry is still seen as dangerous.

From these earliest times through to the medieval Scots makars, to Burns, MacDiarmid and Hamish Henderson, and to the present moment, Scottish poetry has steadfastly refused to tow the state line, shunned the gowns offered by the academy, pledged its troth loyally to the cause of the people. Or it did. More specifically, the attempts by the establishment to reign in the perennial popularity of poetry in Scotland have increased. For this is the age of the literary prize, of 'makars' and 'laureates'.

Despite the undoubted success of many contemporary Scottish novelists, the nineteenth-century bourgeois art form which is the novel has never really been popular in Scotland. One could argue that despite the fact that Walter Scott has done more than anyone to 'invent' the novel as we understand it and to promote the 'one on one' undertaking which reading a novel requires, it still sits uneasily in the gallery of Scottish artistic and social activity, for it is an internal journey not an external trip, an individual experience, not a collective sharing. Charlotte Brontë in *Jane Eyre*, by declaring 'Reader, I married him', is making a mono-cultural assumption as to the individual relationship of the consumer to the work of art.[6] If she were Scottish, she would be more than likely to exclaim 'Listen everybody, I married him! See you at the dance!'

Brontë, one supposes, was writing for a known audience as well as an imagined reader. She was at the same time writing for herself as her target audience and readership were from her known world and class. In Scotland, writers have never strictly written for themselves. By this I mean the writer in Scotland has never been exclusively of themselves, singular or detached. Individual writers may have come and gone, been ignored, denied and died penniless but the main bulwark of Scottish literature is that, like most everything else in Scotland, it is a public activity. This is why poetry and not prose is the art form of the Scottish heart, from Thurso down to the Tweed. Poetry is more of the blood and prose of the mind; one is passion, the other reason.

This idea is not restricted to Scotland, thank goodness. In her moving memoir about her life with her husband, the Russian poet Osip Mandelstam, *Hope Against Hope*, Nadezhda Mandelstam has this to say about the function of the poet

> The work of the poet, as a vehicle for world harmony, has a social character – that is, it is concerned with the doings of the poet's fellow men, among whom he lives and whose fate he shares. He does not speak 'for them', but with them, nor does he set himself apart from them: otherwise he would not be a source of truth.[7]

Whether the reticent nature of the Scot would embrace the Russian idea of the poet 'as a vehicle for world harmony', it is the

---

[6] Charlotte Brontë, *Jane Eyre*, London: Penguin Pocket Classics, 2009.

[7] Nadezhda Mandelstam, *Hope Against Hope*, London: Harvill Press, 1999, p.188.

case that from Dunbar to Liz Lochhead there is a long tradition in Scotland of literary art as being a socialised activity and of having a socialising function. In this way writers have had and still have far more purchase on civic and political life in Scotland than they ever have had in England. In other words there is a sense in Scotland that literature adds to our civilisation as opposed to detracting from it. This latter condition of literature is often the impression one gets when one reads the English press. Perhaps it is going too far to say that England is hostile to imagination and intellect but there definitely is an impression abroad in that land that they are mistrustful of it. A society which relegates it poets to the margins will certainly shiver nervously if they suddenly declare themselves as 'a source of truth'. That kind of 'truth' no government wants to hear.

However, it is worth mentioning here that all critics or propagandists for Scottish poetry must remember how most people in Scotland receive poetry (as opposed to perceiving it) – and this is through the filter of English cultural experience, which is transmitted into the consciousness of the majority of Scots through education. By education I mean here the mandatory 11 years of primary and secondary schooling. By being shackled to the rock of a neighbouring cultural ordering, the common intellectual condition of most people at the end of this process is confusion or apathy. Something has been denied and that 'something' is Scottish literary history which never gets a hearing. Or if it does, the message comes from the occupied space and needs translating.

As Oscar Wilde so famously did not say from the dock but did say as 'Saint Oscar' in Terry Eagleton's play of that name – and here he could be speaking of the Scots as well as the Irish –

> I object to this trial on the grounds that no Irishman can receive a fair hearing in an English court because the Irish are figments of the English imagination. I am not really here; I am just one of your racial fantasies. You cannot manacle a fantasy.[8]

The fantasy prevalent in English Literature, as it is taught in our universities, is that Scottish literature is part of the greater language family of Empire and for that reason has to have a similar

---

[8] Terry Eagleton, *Saint Oscar*, London: Bookmarks, 2004.

genesis and can subsequently be subject to the same hegemonic rules of the literary ascendancy. Scottish poetry, its origin and its cannon, stands in direct opposition to that assumption.

Yet there is little real lasting benefit to be accrued in defining what we are not. Much better for the furtherance of the project is to celebrate what we are by asking and doing. In this undertaking, perversely, we may find that the sturdy vessels of certainty and identity are not as secure as we imagined. There is nothing wrong, creatively, in rocking the boat of assumption.

Maybe the true state of all poets everywhere at anytime is to ask and inhabit the mind-state of John Clare when he wrote 'I am – yet what I am none cares or knows'.[9] The clamour for 'identity', or even recognition, mitigates against this fear of the void – to which Clare felt he was heading (and indeed his destination was the asylum) – and that generalising sump of history where all poets become Anonymous. Contrast this fear with the ready embracing of the Anonymous mask by the 'Occupy the City' movement as their public face. As was Hamish Henderson's reasonable ambition to have his work known, although he was happy enough if it was anthologised as that of 'Anonymous'. For Henderson believed that his work came from and would return to the universal 'carrying stream' of creativity and cultural expression. Contrast the plight of MacDiarmid's life-long struggle in what Norman MacCaig called 'a torchlight procession of one' against the darkness of Clare's exclusion.

What mask does the poet choose now in these quasi-revolutionary times and what duty does the poet have, if any, to the public despite (and because of) all that I have claimed for Celtic cultural inclusiveness? Furthermore, what relationship does the poet have to recent world history as made manifest around the globe through new electronic and cyber technology? As the events in Arab countries unfold – as all future upheavals will be reported, which is through the 'unofficial media' of mobile phones and digi-cameras – does the poet have a role in this unfolding or are poets irrelevant? In what direction exactly is the 'vehicle of world harmony' heading?

This pressure on the poet to have a public function will only increase, and in many ways completes the circle from the

---

9   John Clare, 'I Am', in *John Clare*, London: Dent (Everyman's Poetry), 1997, p.90.

age of bards and skalds to the age of the i-phone. Compounding this frontier – crossing into occupied and unoccupied space is the relentless media driven circus of literary prizes and the fetishising of personality and competition over quality and merit. So it made awkward TV viewing to see John Burnside try to address the question by ignoring it of the inappropriate sponsoring of the T S Eliot poetry prize, which he had just won, by a hedge fund investment company. The reporter had an angle of questioning which the prize winner was either unable or unwilling to answer. £15,000 to a Scottish poet is a fortune. Here was a poet placed in a strange world: in the trivial transience of the saloons of scandal and celebrity; a gaudy, tacky, chemically lit environment but one which nonetheless is firmly in the public domain but which is a place modern poets are not used to being: a literary rabbit in the Warholian headlights of 'fifteen (make that two and a half) minutes of fame'. It was not edifying.

So, in the end, what actually is the difference between the case for the prosecution and the defence of poetry? It could be that the evidence of all the ages of literature's development up to this point is a torchlight procession of one not enough? Maybe we should throw away the telescope and understand what John Muir came to realise about the mountains of Yosemite – that geologically they are always in 'the long now'. This idea is perfectly understood in the theatre which is an art form that exists permanently in the present moment. 'The long now' for an actor is the instant they step on stage to the second they step off. You truly exist as a playwright when your play is being performed; everything else is 'anonymous'.

The ultimate tragedy, I suspect, and the reason poets and poetry occupy a peripheral space in the modern popular consciousness is that the poets whom 'society' rewards have allowed the language of their poems to suffer what William Thomson (or Lord Kelvin as he is more famously known) referred to as 'heat death' in physics. Thomson was trying to formulate some understanding of thermodynamics, of heat and mechanical energy and of how heat loss is a loss of mechanical energy in nature. Applied to the universe this means its ultimate fate is to have diminished to a state of no 'thermodynamic free energy' and 'therefore can no longer sustain motion or life'.[10] A dark gaseous eternity of photon leptons awaits. The timescale for this theory of the heat death of the universe is unimaginably long. So there is no point in worrying about it, rather we should appreciate it as the beauty of physics. The 'heat death' of modern poetry, the loss of linguistic energy, is a far more pressing and anxiety inducing problem for it allows us to appreciate poetry less. How can a poet speak with the people 'among whom he lives', as Nadezhda Mandelstam has it, when there is no linguistic equilibrium, let alone thermodynamics, no give and take, where poetry cannot do its 'work' and where there can be little possibility of the poet becoming 'a vehicle of world harmony'?

If the space in our society reserved for poetry is currently occupied by careerists with a panache for the 'secret language' of safe crackers then it is because we have allowed it to be so occupied. We can, since it is within our collective power, re-possess the space. Who is to say that the government of a newly independent Scotland will be any less or more ambivalent towards culture than the present devolved one? If they saw culture and the arts as being a vital component in the development of the psyche of each individual and hence the nation as opposed to treating it, as they currently do, like a stall at a trade fair or a marketing opportunity then progress could be made. The simple act of the Scottish government buying two thousand copies of each new book of poems by a Scottish poet published in Scotland and distributing them around schools and libraries would go a long way to injecting much needed cash into the moribund beast which is Scottish publishing so that it could at last, to paraphrase W.B. Yeats yet again 'slouch... towards Bethlehem to be born'.[11] It would also put cash in the pockets of Scottish poets and would reduce the need to appear gluff-eyed in the spotlight of public attention. Who knows, they may even get used to it. The poets may even work out for themselves what they are actually for.

---

[10] Lord Kelvin, *On the Dynamical Theory of Heat*, Transactions of the Royal Society of Edinburgh, March, 1851, and Philosophical Magazine IV. 1852.

[11] W B Yeats, 'The Second Coming', *Selected Poems*, London: Penguin Modern Classics, 2000, p.124.

Hamish Henderson and *Broadsheet:*
Putting the Teeth in Context

Hayden Murphy

Context is an imperative in discussing that man of many parts that was Hamish Henderson. His was a compartmentalised series of lives often overlapping but never quite contiguous. It is also important at the start to emphasise I write of a long time friend with whom I was never afraid to differ but rarely disengaged.

Dublin, Grafton Street, June 1966. He is a tall yet to be stooped figure. A figure of kilted swagger and carefully careless demeanour. He is, as far as I recall, in Ireland for first discussions with Garech Browne of Claddagh Records for what, a decade later will become *Freedom Come All Ye: the poems & songs of Hamish Henderson* (1977).

I am introduced by John Ryan in Davy Byrnes bar across the road from the currently being refurbished The Bailey which is owned by John and will be reopened in style in June 1968. We are waiting for Garech to arrive to join us as guests for lunch with John. It is to be a long wait and a very liquid lunch ending up during the 'Holy Hour' in nearby Jammets with plates of oysters before us.

Later in the day, in McDaid's of Harry Street, we met the poet Pearse Hutchison who was briefly back from Barcelona in Dublin to see his mother. There was an edgy competitiveness between the poets. I suspect this may go as far back as 1949 when Hamish, with the proceeds of the Somerset Maugham Poetry Award (for *Elegies for the Dead in Cyrenaica*, 1948), had visited Dublin and, as he said himself 'fell as a sheep among wolves... in other words I met the Behan family.' Pearse had been a close friend of Brendan Behan at around that time. This is supposition. I was never to really know the background of the edginess, but I noticed it again and again when Hamish would meet his literary peers. With musicians and folk in the bar Hamish relaxed. With writers he was often curiously cautious.

Anyway, he went his way and though we exchanged addresses I did not expect to see him again, never mind become a close friend over the next four decades. However, the Edinburgh Festival was to become the catalyst. Later in 1966, after a money-making month in a food-processing factory in Norfolk, I arrived in Edinburgh for the first time. I came via Gloucestershire, where I had given my first professional poetry 'gig', and London, where my good friend the publisher Timothy O'Keeffe had filled me in on Hamish's very distinguished army record and, most significantly for me, the poems that emerged from his experiences. I hunted down copies of John Lehmann's *New Penguin Writing* where the first poems had appeared during the war.

So my first call was to Hamish. He introduced me not only to Sandy Bell's Bar in Forrest Road but also to the nearby bookshop, then being run by Jim Haynes, and down in the Grassmarket the second incarnation of the Traverse Theatre. I was to give readings in both bookshop and theatre and meet not only Scottish poets but also the members of The Scaffold, including Roger McGough.

Then in the company of Hamish, as his guest, I was introduced to the sound of Scots in dramatic circumstances. Douglas Young's *The Burdies* was an 'adaptation and translation' of *The Birds* by Aristophanes. It was the central Drama production in that year's theatre programme at the Royal Lyceum Theatre. The language soared, dipped and dived in ways that were not always understood but always created emotional resonance. I was hooked. As I was by the Festival itself and what R.L. Stevenson called the 'Precipitous City'. In one guise or another; in an audience, performing as a bit player, Director, Front of House Manager, Critic (for over thirty years) I have attended every Festival since. And up to the few years before his death I always did so either in the company of Hamish or, more often, flushed after a meeting with the same man. He was central to my Festival experience.

When in 1971 I brought over from Dublin a Yeats-related two hour one-man piece entitled *The Foul Rag and Bone Shop of the Heart*, Hamish not only welcomed warmly the actor Robert Somerset but in its ten day run attended three times, always bringing at least two guests. The second part of the show was a complete performance of Yeats's great short play *Purgatory*. I played the part of the young boy, a boy who is callously murdered at the end. Robert was robust in the murder scene and once I almost toppled over into the kilted lap of Hamish who always insisted on sitting centre in the front row. This became a lifelong reference point between us.

In February 1967, with my friend Benedict Ryan as my co-editor for the first issue, I launched *Broadsheet* in Dublin. Its international and cosmopolitan intent was a direct result of my experiences the previous year. Particularly in Edinburgh. Hamish was an early subscriber and a great champion of it over the next ten years, though it took some time before I actually got him to contribute a piece for it.

From the mid 1960s, Hamish and I had been active in the Anti-Apartheid movement in our respective countries, particularly in protests against the December 1969 visit by the South African rugby team to Europe and specifically in protests outside, and in Hamish's case inside, the grounds in Dublin and Edinburgh. In 1974, as the British Lions, with a substantial Irish/Scottish contingent, set out to break the sporting embargo on cultural events in South Africa, I asked if I might use Hamish's song 'Rivonia' in *Broadsheet*. There was a problem about copyright. In pragmatic Scottish/Irish accord we changed the title to 'Mandela' and it appeared in *Broadsheet* 22 (December 1974).

Rivonia was the farm where Nelson Mandela and his comrades were arrested and charged with treason in 1963. Hamish composed it after the subsequent trial that sent the leaders of Unkonto we Sizwe (Spear of the Nation) to Robben Island for life. The tune is that of the Spanish republican song of the tragic Spanish Civil War, 'Viva la Quince Brigada'. By the time Atté recorded it for the Claddagh 1977 LP, it had become a widely used piece by such as Pete Seeger and Mick Graves of The Spinners. It was first published under the title 'Rivonia' in the British folksong magazine *Sing* in January 1965.

There was a curious footnote to its appearance in *Broadsheet*. The commissioned artist for that issue was Patrick Graham. His black and white crayon/pencil/wash depiction of The Cage:Kesh (a Concentration Camp in Northern Ireland at the time) attracted the enthusiastic admiration of Hamish. The young Athlone artist was delighted both by the praise and the source of it and amazed me, when on hearing of it, he 'rendered' a true if somewhat tuneless (rather eerily reminiscent of Hamish himself at times) version of the 'John MacLean March'.

Another footnote involves the Irish singer Luke Kelly. In early 1974 he was with myself and Hamish in Sandy Bell's. He launched into a detailed account of his part in the hilarious revival of Brendan Behan's *Richard Cork's Leg* two years earlier. This included the arrival in the second row of the small Peacock Theatre of Kelly's two front teeth following an over enthusiastic version of the 'Old Triangle'. Hamish looked pensive. He was self conscious of his own front teeth which seemed at times to me to be movable objects. Drink and more drink was taken. Luke wanted to sing with Hamish what he referred to as 'that Mandela song'. The opening bars were musically a disaster. Teeth were removed and it appears to me, retrospectively, that all was well for the rest on that long afternoon.

The teeth also figure in a fracas on the opening of Milne's new basement bar in Rose Street in 1982 (I think). Here a simmering row with poet/critic Alan Bold moments after the doors were opened led to the new manager Harry Cullen needing to interpose his body between the by now toothless Hamish and the very corpulent Alan. Cullen, who now manages The Oxford Bar, still pretends to be amazed at all the fuss and import (and pleasure!) I give to recalling that occasion. Joy Hendry, Editor of *Chapman*, gives a somewhat sedate version in the second volume of Tim Neat's splendid biography of Hamish.[1]

Over the years, Hamish had often alluded to a work in progress, *Auld Reekie's Roses*. Depending on the time of day – morning, afternoon, evening, late at night or the following morning – the ambitions for this sequence of poems/songs grew, shrunk, expanded and evaporated. The proposed series never got written.

In January 1974 I was spending a lot of time in both London and Scotland researching the life and works of James Thompson (BV). When in Edinburgh I met Hamish daily. Not always in Sandy Bell's. The alternative was a comparatively quiet pub run by two brothers who revered Hamish (and in later years his splendid dog Sandy) in Drummond Street. Here I saw drafts of 'That Hoor of Dawn', as it became subsequently known in his *Collected Poems and Songs* (Curley Snake 2000). In *Broadsheet 24* (July 1974) it was simply entitled 'Auld Reekie's Roses' and was headed with the music for the 'refrain'. As Thomas Crawford in his informative sleeve notes for the Claddagh record writes. 'this song unites the tradition of urban realism that descends to us from Ramsay and Fergusson'. There is also a spiritual secularism present, particularly in the ambivalence in the refrain 'Lay the lily O' with its various hints at scent, sex and mortality. A feature of the recording is the

---

[1] Timothy Neat, *Hamish Henderson: A Biography, Vol.II, Poetry Becomes People 1952-2002*, Edinburgh: Birlinn, 2009, pp.184-85.

wonderful voice of Alison McMorland. Particularly in the passion she gives to the final verse:

> The wayside pulpit's dredgy
> Can soond for ither lugs.
> The joys o'Heaven we'll leave til
> The angels – and the speugs.

Working from several handwritten versions, I was careful to get the author's approval for the text that appeared in *Broadsheet*. In lineation and spacing it is very different from later versions, but at the time Hamish was so pleased that he was to be seen selling copies across the city during that year's Festival. I was nearly always with him, which is how we came to see the unique production of Sean McCarthy's *The Fantastical Feats of Finn MacCool* twice in the Haymarket Ice Rink. While I gazed in wonder at Hamish Imlach appearing, thanks to a fortified forklift, out of a very narrow door half-way up the wall at one end of the rink, Hamish seemed very focused on the bare torso and mermaid scaled Jeanne Crowley slithering along the ice towards an imperious Johnny Bett. We both enjoyed the marvellous sound of Planxty and also attended their individual concert performance towards the end of the 'play's' run.

Christy Moore, with Planxty at the time, was to remember this as an early meeting with Hamish. Earlier this year Christy (whom I have known since his Dublin days in the '60s) wrote to me:

> memory is a strange thing with me... around the songs I seem to have almost total recall... other dimensions vary in recall... my memories of Hamish H are those of a tall kind man very interested in the songs and their singers.. I mainly met him in Sandy Bell's but also at Blairgowrie Festival and in various Folk Clubs.

My abiding memory of the two of them is in March 1983 when Christy stayed over a day to visit an exhibition with me in the National Library of Scotland, and from there we went to meet Hamish and others in the pub. Songs were sung, and even the impatient barking suggesting a wish to go home by Hamish's dog Sandy was ignored. The 'craic' was good.

That issue of *Broadsheet* back in 1974 had a distinct and deliberate Scottish tone to it, and Hamish was delighted to share space with fellow drinkers from Sandy Bell's such as Geordie Hamilton and Tony C McManus.

Between 1975-1978, apart from brief stays in Barcelona and Berlin, I moved between Dublin, London and Edinburgh. Often I was the go-between for London publishers Martin, Brian & O'Keeffe and Chris Grieve (Hugh MacDiarmid), both delivering and collecting proofs for the two volume *Complete Poems of Hugh MacDiarmid* (1978) from the author in the cottage in Brownsbank, Biggar he shared with his wife Valda Trevlyn until his death on 9 September 1978. Being aware of a long standing competitive frisson between Hamish and Chris, I was wary of discussing one with the other though I was present when they met in amiable and convivial sessions at two celebratory occasions in Edinburgh itself.

I also, vividly, recalled Hamish's reaction to first reading *Lucky Poet* (1943) two years after its publication in Merano, Italy. In the poem 'To Hugh MacDiarmid on Reading Lucky Poet' Hamish concludes somewhat belligerently:

> Amidst all the posturings, tantrums and rages,
> Is there something you haven't said, in all these pages?
> Is there some secret room, and you don't want to show it?
> Did an unlucky break befall the Lucky Poet?[2]

MacDiarmid's funeral took place on 13 September in Langholm. Tim Neat, Hamish's future biographer, drove him, myself and Timothy O'Keeffe there and back from Edinburgh. Mist, drizzle and later gale force winds and rain accompanied us. On the way back Hamish insisted we cut off the main route and visit the cemetery at Crowdieknowe.[3] This was both burial ground of generations of Grieveses and also the subject of MacDiarmid's great poem simply entitled after the place itself. As three of us sheltered under nearby trees and a useless shared umbrella, Hamish mounted a gravestone and declaimed:

> Oh to be at Crowdieknowe
> When the last trumpet blaws,

---

[2] Hamish Henderson, 'To Hugh MacDiarmid', *Collected Poems and Songs*, edited by Raymomd Ross, Edinburgh: Curly Snake, 2000, p. 120.

[3] Hugh MacDiarmid, *Selected Poetry*, edited by Alan Riach and Michael Grieve, New York: New Directions, 1993, p.14.

An' see the dead come loupin' owre
The old grey wa's

Hamish was not really up to 'loupin' but there seemed to come an answering thunder crash from the sky as he concluded

An' glower at God an' a' his gang.

Recalling that occasion, as one of Hamish's selected alternative 'gang', is but one of many memorable moments that make his friendship so alive and active in memory.

During these years I was also privileged to be allowed to work with Hamish on several drafts of the poem 'Floret silva undique' (woodlands flourish everywhere) which he would refer to as 'maybe the second or the fourth of the *Auld Reekie's Roses* sequence I am determined to get done'. Sadly it was not to be. The proposed and often promised protracted sequence never materialised, though the poem itself was read by the poet himself on the 1977 Claddagh record. However he was determined to see his text in 'proper print' and honoured me by giving me the slightly amended version for *Broadsheet 26-30* (16 June 1978). Here he entitled it 'Auld Reekie's Roses II' and gave his own translation of the opening line as 'the wood is flowering all about'.

Here again sex and death are the central themes and characters. As is Edinburgh itself: 'Reekie's oot for a Sabbath stroll.' Some sections are set in the Meadows near Hamish's own home in Melville Terrace. In section two, 'Death', called by his medieval nickname 'Sma'back', appears alive and kicking in Greyfriars' Kirkyard. In the Grassmarket, beneath the Castle, 'toun and tour/The gowans gay and the gilliefloor'. And in the end, glorious and triumphant, 'Flora is queen of lusty May.'

For both poems in their *Broadsheet* versions Hamish generously gave a glossary for some of the Scots words/phrases. I do not think these necessary for readers of this piece.

Following the launch of the final issue in Dublin, London and Edinburgh I started to plan a permanent move to Edinburgh. In late March 1979 I settled in Clarence Street in the New Town part of the city. Fergus Lenihan, feature editor in *The Irish Times*, created an 'Arts in Scotland Correspondent' role for me. Fintan O'Toole, followed by Ciaran Carty, delegated Festival duties to me for *The Sunday Tribune.* Novelist John Banville was my Dublin Editor for exclusive coverage of the Book Festival (which started in 1983) in the weekend literary pages of *The Irish Times*.

So, in August 1980, I was able to repay Hamish's hospitality of 1966 and bring him as my honoured guest to Bill Bryden's unforgettable two-part adaptation of the York/Wakefield Mystery plays, collectively entitled *The Passion* and staged in promenade fashion in the Assembly Hall. It was the highlight of that year's Festival. An abiding memory is of Hamish, hat forever on head, leading a rotating conga of dancers to the pulsating rhythms of the Albion Band, led to glorious musical heights by Hamish's own great interpreter of his songs and ballads, Alison McMorland.

However, *Broadsheet* and Hamish's involvement both with and in it was not quite over. In early 1982 my friend Larry Hutchison (teacher and Antiquarian) and his friend Max Begg (Librarian NLS) introduced me to Dr Anne Matheson, the Exhibitions Officer in the National Library of Scotland. She was interested in mounting a retrospective exhibition of *Broadsheet: 1967-1978: Poetry, Prose & Graphics*. A Bursary was given by the Scottish Arts Council, and for over a year I worked with artist/restorer Janet Lawson in framing, mounting and cataloguing 227 items from the issues over the years. On 3 February 1983 the exhibition was opened by Edwin Morgan and ran until the summer of that year. To mark the occasion, I edited and produced a special single page issue of *Broadsheet*. Hamish, naturally, was included among the eighteen invited poets/contributors.

Since 1972, my host when visiting Edinburgh had been the English teacher Kate Ballantyne. Our relationship was comfortably easy going. In 1981 we got married, but the demands of marriage destroyed the relationship and within years we were living apart. We divorced in 1988. However, in 1981 Hamish gifted us with two poems, in his own unique translations, and with, I think, a revealing and important introduction.

Under the general title 'Of Eros and of Dust', the poems were 'Tomb of Iases' by C.P.Cavafy (1853-1933) and 'Chimaera' by Dino Campana (1885-1932). He introduced them thus:

These two translations together form a kind of janus-poem. I seldom think of the one without thinking of the other. They seem to me to express the psycho-sexual ambivalence of much poetic creativity, the interpenetrative ambiguity of its very nature.

In this short statement he seems to me to be giving a brilliant précis of his own general, generous and humane approach not only to poetry but to the creative force that was his lifetime's focus. In the exhibition *Broadsheet* I published the Dino Campana translation containing the evocative lines:

> I, poet of the night,
> kept vigil over the bright stars
> in the oceans of the sky.[4]

On 9 March 2002, aged 82, Hamish died in Edinburgh. The evening after hearing of his death I was walking across the Meadows to an event in Cross Causewayside. Out of the Spring haar came a dog with a ball in its mouth. It dropped the ball at my feet and in mock challenge bared its teeth and invited me to be part of its game. I was facing towards Melville Terrace and I swear I could hear a shout from afar, 'Sandy'. In the shape of the trees emerged a head with a hat. Cheshire Cat style. Behind came another set of protruding teeth, a familiar face with a familiar smile. As ever with Hamish, context was all.

---

[4] Hamish Henderson, 'Chimaera', *Collected Poems and Songs*, p. 124.

Sectarian Songs
The Hamish Henderson Lecture 2011

Owen Dudley Edwards

I

Nowadays it is customary for the year's deliverer of a Lecture named in someone's honour to open with some words on the speaker's acquaintanceship friendship/discipleship with the Lecture-Name's owner or, alternatively, with regrets for the speaker's lack of same, but with testimony to the ideological/intellectual/imaginative personal debt to the owner of the name.

I admire the practice, even if I am about to send it up rotten, and I prefer it for the chief reasons Hamish Henderson would have preferred it: that the older, more refined, more genteel academic habit was to revere the name and forget its holder, and that the lecturer who forgets the godpaternity – or the god – of her/his lecture is inexorably losing her/his own identity, and reducing the identity of the lecture series to an advertising-agent's brand-name.

I knew Hamish Henderson so well that we were not on speaking terms for sixteen years.

I first heard of him from my lifelong friend Denis Tuohy, telling me of his experiences as lead actor with the Irish Festival Players in 1958, he from Queen's Belfast, most if not all of the rest from Trinity College Dublin. To Denis the Edinburgh Festival (seen whence he saw it, on the as yet small Fringe) came into focus through the prism that was Hamish Henderson.

That Hamish would take the earliest opportunity of seeing the Irish Festival Players was inevitable. They were performing Yeats plays; they thus reflected a culture (either original or educated) saturated in folklore; they were youthful, and would perform some heroic roles, such as Cuchulainn; at least some of them, whether actors or actresses, would be beautiful or handsome. Denis Tuohy was handsome if firmly heterosexual. He was studying for a degree in Classics in his native Belfast. He was a Catholic and could therefore be informative on the Unionist oppression of Catholics, and Hamish, still within the Communist orbit, was firmly hostile to the partition of Ireland. On the other hand, Denis might be expected to know Ulster songs, Catholic and perhaps even Protestant. One can see the collector's eye gleaming at the prospects of what he might collect.

It was no more than an ordinary friendship, whatever Hamish's other hopes for it. And Denis, while wary, was fascinated by Hamish. Through Hamish's eyes he discovered the Festival in its potential realities, and the greater Scotland behind it. Both Edinburgh and its Festival might show symptoms of Laputa life: to imagine oneself in a flying island, poised over southeastern Scotland, perhaps observing it from time to time but never touching it. Hamish was romantic, but as any reader of his *Elegies* must agree, his was the romanticism of realities. Denis returned to Ireland and went forward to a major London career in TV news and culture, but retaining a vision of Edinburgh and its Festival on the ground, if somewhat enchanted ground, as expounded by a fascinating giant.

I came to Edinburgh University as a Lecturer in History in 1968, the year of James Connolly's birth centenary. Desmond Greaves, the Communist historian and journalist, had established year and place (Edinburgh) in the teeth of previous assumptions. Hamish took a major part in fixing a commemorative plaque in the Cowgate, then slightly, but only slightly, brighter than Connolly had known it as the child whose father fed the family from the meagre wages the city gave him for spading horse-dung from the streets after the day's traffic. The boy could look up from the darkness of Cowgate slums to the wealthy thoroughfares South Bridge and George IV Bridge bounding over them: he could see and suffer the class system in street levels before he could read a line of Marx or Engels whom he would later apply so dramatically to the writing of *Labour in Irish History* and whose relevance to Irish nationalism he finally and vainly sought to drive home by being shot for leading socialists and nationalists in the Easter Week Rising of 1916. Hamish and I automatically assumed each other's admiration for Connolly and enjoyed comparing what each of us had learned from the evidence of surviving contemporaries in my native Dublin and his Edinburgh. He was the soul of generosity in giving me tapes or talks, and his love of Connolly and what Connolly represented lit up his whole being as he talked. He never lost the childlike eagerness at discovery, and seemed to turn anew to whatever excited him.

There was a divine light in his eye, and his parted lips savoured the wonders to be found in the living dead. (Quite right, they are our vampires and can only survive on our generous blood.)

We ceased to be on speaking terms when I was Director of the Scottish Universities Summer School in July 1970. Our visiting lecturer for 24 hours was an eminent scholar in Scottish Studies from out of town; he had lectured well, interested his audience, many from the USA, the European continent, and Asia. He promised to meet enthusiasts at 10.00pm at our HQ, Carlyle Hall. He arrived back five hours after the appointed hour, and I was angry with him and the obvious cause of the destructive delay, Hamish, both of them belligerently pickled. I was pompous in my reproaches. The lady with them, Dolina Maclennan, was hitherto unknown to me, and said simply: "You are angry. And you may be right to be angry. But I will sing to you now, and then you will cease to be angry." She sang. She was quite right. I remember my anger melting away like snow. But, alas, by that time Hamish had departed, after characterising me with a startling accuracy, however unflattering in its terms. The diplomatic desert which now lay between us was to be interrupted by three oases.

The first was in 1974 when Gordon Brown (then graduate student for a history doctorate and Rector of the University, to the great annoyance of Principal Sir Michael Swann) was a main spirit and former and future Chair of the Edinburgh University Students' Publications Board (locally known as Pubs Board). Amongst its other publications was the *New Edinburgh Review*, originally regular but now in the hands of a truculent Trotskyite who dismissed any supervision or attempts to tie him to the regular appearance of the journal as the Scottish Arts Council reasonably preferred. The journal initially had advisers from the professorial community of its choice (James Cornford in Politics, Aubrey Manning in Zoology) but these had been disappeared; my growing friendships with Gordon Brown and other students on the Board led to my co-option annually from 1974 to 1980. Hamish became aware of this, and conscripted me as a messenger-boy, as indifferent as myself to our nominal distance, in the light of emergency. My part in the successful operation following conscription was of minimal importance, save possibly as a final feather liberating the journal from its guard (in the end by becoming guest editor for a couple of issues). But what I discovered was that Hamish had from the first played the decisive part in an intellectual revolution which would ultimately bring about Scottish Devolution. It arose first from his love for Gordon Brown. 'Love' is the right word, love and nothing more, Gordon firmly heterosexual: I apologise for the crassness of this explication but press witch hunts against Gordon Brown have left no possible slur unspoken. Contradictory to press lynch-mobs' portraits, Gordon Brown was one of the most courteous, charming, amusing, good-natured, considerate, appreciative and delightful companions any of his faculty or student acquaintances at Edinburgh knew. It was in fact his seemingly indestructible good nature that had caused the crisis requiring Hamish to resurrect me. Hamish's war and postwar work in Italy and in Italian Africa led him to discover Antonio Gramsci.

World War II propaganda told English speaking peoples that nationalism was a root-cause of Nazism (as National Socialism's name declared), Italian Fascism, &c, plus minor undesirables like Irish neutrality. The thesis was self-contradictory, based on the fundamental assumption that nationalism was something only the other fellow did, when in fact English nationalism, and its occasional synonym British nationalism, had provided so much of the truly heroic spirit with which the UK defied Hitler. In the USA, American nationalism was divided between isolationism and self-defence by international alliance. Jews saw the mass murder of so many of their people as the product of nationalism. Stalin had amused himself by playing theoretical games with a ration of local national consciousness but in practice was out to crush nationalism whether it showed itself in the USSR or Communist parties elsewhere. Churchill's war leadership assumed the UK's heroism was in defence of Empire as well as country, and dangers to Empire stemmed from nationalism in the countries the Empire ruled. Irish nationalism in its most extreme form, the IRA, was in alliance with Hitler and sought to give him an Irish foothold to threaten the UK. Saunders Lewis, the founder of Plaid Cymru, had intellectual sympathies with Fascism. The Scottish National Party had no such affiliation, but some of its prominent figures went to jail rather than be conscripted in a war to which Scottish consent had never been sought (while most if not all SNP prisoners would probably have agreed that had Scots been asked for their consent to the war, they would have given it). Ideals of international Socialism made the British Labour party really hostile to Scottish and Welsh nationalism (heavy Irish-born support in British elections blunted their public dislike of the Irish variety), and Communist propaganda opposed the British retention of Northern Ireland. Aneurin Bevan and his wife Jennie Lee were obvious symbolic representatives of Scottish and Welsh industrial culture but, if anything, their Scottishness and Welshness made them more vociferous against local nationalisms. The Labour party's founders had included Scottish nationalists, notably R. B. Cunninghame Graham, but after the war the party dropped its traditional support for Scottish Home Rule.

   Timothy Neat's invaluable and painstaking biography of Hamish Henderson makes it clear that Hamish's own postwar sojourn in Ulster distanced him from left-wing anti-nationalist orthodoxies. Northern Ireland Communism, having no chance of alliance with Unionist Labour, kept nibbling at the fringes of the IRA with no greater welcome than British Communism got from the greater part of its target for conversion, the Labour party. Scottish Communism, theoretically Hamish's ideological home at this point, was as bitterly hostile to Scottish nationalism as the Labour party would like, and had expelled Christopher Murray Grieve aka Hugh MacDiarmid for his demand that Scottish nationalism be accepted as compatible (and indeed essential) to Communism. (Hence, when the party haemorrhaged after the USSR repression in Hungary in 1956, MacDiarmid charged back in since the Communists did not dare to reject him now, however much they deplored the nationalism he forcibly fed them.) Hamish by 1951 had been fascinated by Scotland's nationalist Communist John Maclean (1879-1923) but was also impressed by the literary Catholic Scots nationalist Moray MacLaren in his Penguin paperback *The Scots*. But with all due respect to MacDiarmid, MacLaren, Maclean and James Connolly, the massive nationalist intellectual impact on Hamish was made by the letters of Antonio Gramsci which Hamish translated over the next two decades, and to which he converted Gordon Brown.

   None of Gordon Brown's biographers have understood his early intellectual beliefs, and even the most thorough of them, Paul Routledge, merely referred to Gramsci as being an 'obligatory' reference when Brown wrote his essay in his anthology of new Scottish Socialist essays, *The Red Paper on Scotland* (1975). On this showing, Mr Routledge might refer to Galileo's making 'obligatory references' to Copernicus when addressing the Inquisition. *The Red Paper* came into existence because the Henderson text of Gramsci had shown Gordon Brown that nationalism was compatible with Socialism. In so doing, it left him vulnerable to brutal denunciation from the orthodox Scottish Labour *apparatchiks* of 1974, some

of whom reduced him to tears (Helen Liddell, pathologically anti-
nationalist, seemed to be auditioning for the Wicked Witch of the
West in *The Wizard of Oz* (variants of 'I'll get you and your little dog
Gramsci too')). All politicians anticipate charges of opportunism,
most of them by being opportunist. The SNP capture of 7 seats
in the February 1974 election, and 11 in the October one, led
Harold Wilson to take devolution seriously (Heath and Douglas-
Home having somewhat preceded him in its discovery). But the
Gramsci infection had already been sped on its way by Hamish
years before, and he had succeeded in godfathering a Gramsci
conference at Edinburgh under EUSPB guidance, with the promise
of publication well before the SNP had more than one seat. The
original overture to Gordon had most appropriately been in
the Meadow Bar, then pubs board's favourite pub (although of
course subsequent discussions were held in Hamish's headquarters
in Sandy Bell's, then officially entitled the Forrest Hill Bar, a name
de rigeur never to be used). But between the two of them,
Hamish and Gordon sent Gramsci-consciousness seething through
Edinburgh University staff and students alike, and recruited others
already versed in Gramsci but celebrating him chiefly in little-read
publications. Probably no Edinburgh Rector had done so much for
the University's intellectual life since Rosebery in 1880-83 (later
another unhappy Prime Minister to be undervalued by the English,
although respected by the Scots). The absurd George Robertson,
as ludicrously shallow as the Kailyard of Scottish politics could
spawn, claimed Devolution had been created to destroy the SNP.
What Hamish and Gordon sought to do was to extend and enrich
intellectual discussion whence the best conclusions could be drawn:
the Red Paper, for instance, included left-wingers from a range of
political perspectives, including SNP. But before it could take full
shape, the Gramsci letters and appropriate scholarly discussion
had to be published, and that meant stirring the Trotskyite editor
from his self-admiring throne. Gordon's anxiety to respect his
colleagues had kept him from harassing the nominal enabler of
Gramsci publication. Pubs Board denizens were cheerfully rude
to one another, whatever our academic status, but an anchorite
cocooned in self-protective vituperation was less easy to deal with
(he classified the Board as 'a gaggle of arty-farties' in the editorial
of his final number of the Gramsci papers when it was finally
gouged out of him). Gordon, always gentle in student relations,
recoiled from envenomed controversy in his own back yard as

well as in the Labour party soviets. I suspect that if he afterwards got a name for harsh dictation it was because he wanted to see as little as possible of internal hostilities and harshness seemed a short-cut to conclusion. But the importance of Hamish's influence on Gordon was far more than steps on the road to 10 Downing Street: it was the first decisive move in rank and file party politics to bringing a major party back to Home Rule. Gordon's championship of devolution won friends for its conviction and courage, and made the cause a national one where up to then it had been limited to some SNP and Liberals. And Hamish did it because of his pride in the doctrine of national self-respect, firmly allied to the brotherhood of humankind, and because he thought Gordon a charming and courageous young man. When he called on me to help clear the editorial log-jam, he stressed that I must make it clear he willingly gave all his rights in the publication and would not take a penny for his twenty years' labour. All Scots should be proud of them both, they got us where we are, constitutionally, by opening up the terrain. They were brave.

The second oasis in 1977 was a long-term result of the first. Gordon had moved into academic and journalistic life (springboarding to Scottish statesmanship) but I was still on Pubs Board where Hamish's *Elegies for the Dead in Cyrenaica* was now to be republished with Hamish's continued insistence that the Board should take all the profits. It was as if in the living students to whom he gave his elegies, the dead he mourned could be resurrected. (Neither he, nor the nominally atheist MacDiarmid, would have repudiated the Christlike imagery.) What we made of the book individually I cannot say, but I think all of us were silenced in wonder. Many of us knew World War I poetry (I had guest-lectured on it for Open University History) and had no sense of such stature as Sassoon and Owen and above all Rosenberg being discoverable in the Second World War. World War I was a soldier's war, World War II a people's. Hamish for us was the soldier poet, because of his universalism of perception and suffering, and the extraordinary beauty of his verse which gritted desert sands between its readers' teeth and found the sublime in the loneliness of combat. The Sassoons and Owens and Rosenbergs would have known he was theirs. *Elegies* rescued German dead from shame, British from oblivion. Publishing it left us feeling in a strange twilight world. It was a heavenly honour to be given poems of such stature, intimacy and wonder. We looked out old reviews to cite. But why was it not permanently in print from some poetry publisher, as the comparable Wilfred Owens and Siegfried Sassoons were, this epiphany for eternity hailed at first appearance by (English) critics for its 'real quality and power'?[1]

I had a more pivotal and disreputable role in the third oasis, to which Timothy Neat's invaluable biography is the obvious introduction:

> 'Invisibility' has always been one of Hamish's cultural weapons, and the success of his silent 'underground methodology' is well illustrated by the little-known collaboration Hamish enjoyed with the historian Ted Cowan. In 1979 – as he set out on what would become a distinguished academic career – Edward J. Cowan was commissioned to edit an alternative history of Scotland, *The People's Past – Scottish Folk, Scottish History* (EUSPB 1980). Cowan planned the book in collaboration with Hamish and, although the book is very much Cowan's, Hamish's contribution was important. Hamish wrote the opening essay, the keynote essay, and the poetical postscript that rounds the book out. On publication, *The People's Past* was received with considerable enthusiasm and helped make Cowan's reputation. Today, Cowan is Professor of Scottish History at Glasgow University and his philosophical framework as a historian remains very close to that originally defined by Hamish. [2]

---

[1] *New Statesman and Nation*, 2 April 1949.

2 Timothy Neat, *Hamish Henderson: A Biography, Vol.II, Poetry Becomes the People*, Edinburgh: Birlinn, 2009, pp. 317-18. In fact, by 1979 Ted Cowan's academic career was already highly distinguished as Lecturer in Scottish History at the University of Edinburgh both as a manly (in every sense) combatant in Scottish historiographical wars in the 1970s, which so vigorously advanced the subject and entertained the spectators, and as the author of the foremost historical study of the Civil Wars general Montrose, which the critic for the *Scottish Historical Review* said was not the definitive work only because no book ever could be. When I interviewed Max Hastings (the future editor of great London newspapers) on his immediately previous life of Montrose, Hastings, to his honour, said that his book would only last until Ted Cowan's appeared, for that would have mastery of the indispensible Gaelic sources incomprehensible to Hastings.

In 1980, the Chair of Edinburgh Student Publications Board (about to be rebaptised as Polygon) was Bruce Young, at 26 senior to most of the Board, with some years' journalistic experience, but looking little more than a wise 18, handsome, heterosexual and studying English literature (and subsequently BBC Scotland's Senior Talks Producer). He was dismayed to have to tell us that Ted Cowan, having brought together what would prove less than two-thirds of the original essays, had had to depart for his new post at what was rapidly becoming North America's leading academic centre of Scottish Studies, Guelph University, Toronto, Ontario, Canada; that he had been promised work from Hamish Henderson and Norman Buchan, MP, and hoped we could find some way of getting them to produce it, although he himself had not had one line. If we got the missing essays, the book would have to be expertly edited by a folklorist. I remarked that my wife Bonnie had had a degree from the University of Pennsylvania in English and folklore under the great folklorist MacEdward Leach, that she had worked on copy-editing (and rewriting) historical, literary and other essays for an Irish-American Bicentennial (1976) volume, and that I thought she would have time to do what work was necessary, knowing there could be no remuneration. She agreed and started work, and we confronted the problem of absent friends, friends not to me, I stressed, but certainly friends to the book, however delinquent. It was not that I was not on speaking terms with Norman Buchan: the problem was more likely to be to get the speaking to stop on any occasion when we were together, I being SNP and Norman as hard-hitting a Labour Party champion as any of its ex-Communists could prove. As a matter of fact I was very fond of him, having had to preview for the *Radio Times* many of his inspirational programmes on folksong, *For Johnnie Sangster*, whence I knew what fine work his essay would be. Norman (and there was a touch of the Old Testament prophet in him) might anathemise the unrepentant sinner, but I suspected would be kindness and courtesy themselves if approached by the sinner's wife. And so it proved. Amidst his heavy work as a constituency MP and Opposition spokesman against the Thatcherite nightmare, Norman made Bonnie welcome and rapidly disgorged a sparkling discussion of folksong in history. Peace broke out between us, and I look back with gratitude on our last meeting when we hugged and kissed goodbye.

In the case of Hamish it was of course once more a question of sending my wife into the line of battle instead of myself, since (a) she was effectively the editor until publication day, and (b) she was not known to Hamish who would thus be unable to plead the pressures which Auld Acquaintance would understand or, for that matter, to take refuge in the vow of silence in diplomatic relations. But more than one conscript was needed. I told Bruce Young that since Hamish's would certainly be the cornerstone of the book (regardless of its being the last to arrive) we would need the Board's Chair as well as the Board's internal editor. I watched my troops march off with something more than the austerity of a desert General, and worked at the Board while awaiting the mission's return.

This announced itself by the arrival of Bruce Young: "Did you know Hamish Henderson was gay when you sent me to see him?"

"Yes."

"Bastard!"

I bowed my head in modest acknowledgement of this unreserved tribute to my statesmanship. Bonnie and he then burst virtually into song, possibly not classifiable under any of the varieties dissected by Norman Buchan. Hamish was truly happy to meet Bonnie and talk folklore, but the sight of Bruce apparently elicited immediate assurances of not just the one essay (which was all we could hope for) but the promise of delivery (before any other task on hand) of two, and (on reflection) even three. And not so much as a phone-call was necessary after that. Bruce and Bonnie brought the new material into form as camera-ready copy, Ted Cowan sent a most appreciative acknowledgment of their editing for inclusion, and Scotland had launched a new historical dimension. Shortly after my arrival at Edinburgh in 1968 I heard the admirable but orthodox Sir Herbert Butterfield lecturing that folklore would of course not be used by any reputable historian. I revere him, but as a historian of Ireland and of the USA I knew how invaluable folklore was proving to history there. It was a particular delight to see it now acquire its place of centrality in the writing of Scottish history, where it remains.

Every true Shakespeare needs his Mr W. H.

© Allan McMillan

II

The formal resumption of speaking terms between Hamish Henderson and myself was achieved in 1986 in circumstances appropriate for us both, we being teachers. My daughter Leila began an Honours degree – Scottish Studies and English Literature – at Edinburgh and told me she was now studying with Hamish Henderson and he was a darling. Naturally, it is not possible to continue in mutual silence when one man's daughter is culturally enchanted by the other's teaching, and I ran up to Hamish to thank him for the delight he was giving her, and this was received by a beam in which all hostility vanished. We were thankful that our reconciliation had so gratifying a basis.

Leila's second class with Hamish began with the class's return to the designated room in Scottish Studies telling how it has been enthralled with the first class, but in tributes flowing in the absence of the master. After about ten minutes, an experienced votary said there was no point in wasting further time and the class should adjourn to Sandy Bell's, where he must be. They did, and he was. He beamed at them without the slightest embarrassment, if anything in surprise at their expecting a lecture, but if they wished one he would not disappoint them. So he bought them all drinks, eyed Leila, and commenced: "You are a Papist. I will therefore sing 'The Ould Orange Flute'." Which he did, and which they loved. What Sandy Bell, or his representatives, thought of this transformation of their premises into lecture-hall and concert-hall simultaneously we cannot say, but clearly he had them well trained.

Hamish correctly assumed that Leila would be amused, charmed and instructed by his singing, and that so would I – his assurance as to her Papishness also assumed that. He and I might have made rude remarks about one another, but we would never have been guilty of the insult of assuming the other lacked a sense of humour.

Like Hamish, though regardless of the religion of the reader, I will now provide 'The Ould Orange Flute'. It has many versions, differing in little of importance, and mine is established among them with scansion to the music as determinant:

The Ould Orange Flute

In the County Tyrone, near the town of Dungannon,
Where many the ruction myself had a hand in,
Bob Williamson lived there – a weaver by trade,
And all of us thought him a stout Orange blade.
On the twelfth of July as it yearly did come,
Bob played on the flute to the sound of the drum.
You may talk of your harp, your piano, or lute,
But there's nothing to sound like the ould Orange flute.

Now, Bob, the deceiver, he took us all in,
For he married a Papish called Bridget McGinn,
Turned Papish himself, and forsook the old cause,
That gave us our freedom, religion, and laws.
Now, the boys in the place made some comment upon it,
And Bob had to fly to the province of Connaught;
He fled with his wife and his fixings to boot,
And along with the rest took the ould Orange flute.

At the chapel on Sunday to atone for past deeds,
He said Paters and Aves and counted his beads,
Till after some time at the Priest's own desire,
He went with his ould flute to play in the choir;
He went with his ould flute to play in the Mass,
But the instrument shivered and sighed, 'Oh, alas!'
When try as he would, though it made a great noise,
The flute would play only, 'The Protestant Boys'.

Bob jumped and he started and got in a splutter,
And threw the ould flute in the blessed holy water;
He thought that this charm would bring some other sound,
When he tried it again, it played 'Croppies Lie Down'.

And for all he could whistle and finger and blow,
To play Papish music he found it no go,
'Kick the Pope', and 'Boyne Water', such like it would
    sound
But one Papish squeak in it couldn't be found.

At the council of priests that was held the next day,
They decided to banish the ould flute away,
Since they couldn't knock heresy out of its head,
They bought Bob another to play in its stead.
So the ould flute was doomed, and its fate was pathetic,
'Twas fastened and burned at the stake as heretic;
As the flame roared around it they heard a brave noise
Twas the ould flute still whistling 'The Protestant Boys'.

Timothy Neat fortunately obtained the text of Paul Nolan's
interview of Hamish in 1998, recalling Northern Ireland as he knew
it between 1945 and 1955:

> A song like 'The O[u]ld Orange Flute' was not then just an
> anti-Catholic song; it was a song, and to me that song gave
> expression to myths and forces going back thousands of
> years – to Orpheus, to the world of Apollo and Marsyas ...[3]

The best criticism is that which opens up doors the reader of
the text has failed to discern. Here Hamish shakes us free of
the pejorative present, and makes us realise we are looking at
something incredibly old. Shakespeare (or possibly Fletcher)
summed up the Orpheus tradition in the Song sung to Queen
Katherine of Aragon in *King Henry VIII*, III.i.3-14:

> Orpheus with his lute made trees,
> And the mountain-tops that freeze,
> Bow themselves, when he did sing:
> To his music plants and flowers
> Ever sprung; as sun and showers
> There had made a lasting spring.

---

[3] Timothy Neat, *Hamish Henderson: A Biography, Vol. I: The Making of the Poet, 1919-1953*, Edinburgh: Birlinn, 2007, p. 225.

> Every thing that heard him play,
> Even the billows of the sea,
> Flung their heads, and then lay by.
> In sweet music is such art,
> Killing care and grief of heart
> Fall asleep, or hearing, die.

(It probably was Fletcher.) We have to take it a stage further and see trees, mountain-tops, plants, flowers, billows &c performing in Orpheus's manner when he had been killed. Or we could think of Wilde's poem in prose, 'The Disciple', about the pool in which Narcissus saw his own image from whose contemplation he could never tear himself away, but when he was dead the pool mourned his loss since it said it had seen its own beauty mirrored in his eyes. Marsyas, flayed alive by Apollo for daring to claim his flute-playing superior to Apollo's music, became a stream in which one could hear his flute still playing. The unknown poet was even thinking of a lute like Orpheus's, if only as a rhyme for the Flute, thus strengthening Hamish's case for classical mythological antecedents. Marsyas's flute must be the most famous in world legend.

But of course the imagery nearest to the poet and his audience would be the Protestant martyrs of Mary Tudor's persecution – Thomas Cranmer, Hugh Latimer, Nicholas Ridley... Wordsworth's Ecclesiastical Sonnet XXXV 'Cranmer' follows its version of the death by fire

> Then, 'mid the ghastly ruins of the fire,
> Behold the unalterable heart entire,
> Emblem of faith untouched, miraculous attestation![4]

This raises an alarming question. It is hard not to sing 'The Ould Orange Flute' without a thrill for the Flute's courage and constancy at the end, but at the same moment it is hard not to laugh at the absurdity: to summon up a unity of such warring emotions is a remarkable poetic feat. There is an element of satire at the expense of the Marian victims coexisting with homage to them, particularly Latimer, whose constancy outshone that of his colleagues. This even prompts the appalling thought that the

---

[4] William Wordworth, 'Ecclesiastical Sonnets', *The Collected Poems of William Wordsworth*, London: Wordworth, 1994, p.521.

whole song is a Papist conspiracy in which innocent Orangemen have been trapped for centuries. Apart from making an example of the Flute (which presumably they felt could not suffer) the priests do not come out badly, and many a Catholic singing the song must have felt Bob Williamson was exceptionally fortunate in his Connacht priest paying for the new flute, instead of defraying the replacement from the wretched refugee's thin coffers. The imagery of the Protestant faith receiving testimony from an inanimate object is sinisterly akin to Gaelic Jacobite poems such as Piaras MacGearailt's *'Rosc Catha na Mumhan'* (the Battle-song of Munster) where the return of the exiled Stuart still hoped for in the early 1740s is signalled by rejoicing bird-song, music from the tops of trees, superior light from sun and moon, and exultation from the fairies. It would be a nice business if a song suspected of Protestant sectarianism turned out to be the product of a Catholic variety. But however electrifying and even entertaining, the thesis will not stand. No Irish Catholic would have referred to what we call the 'Our Father' and the 'Hail Mary' as 'Pater' and 'Ave'. Protestants assume us to be more Romanised than we are. The popular folk-song 'Danny Boy' reveals the same thing when Danny's girlfriend or boy-friend hopes that in the event of the singer's death Danny will say an 'Ave': it was of course an ecumenical Englishman who wrote it, Fred Weatherly, adapting his text to 'The Londonderry Air' for authenticity, unaware that that form is Breton rather than Irish (probably picked up by a Derry sailor from a Breton fellow-fisherman on the Iceland beat).

But to revert to Hamish's unquestionably accurate diagnosis of a classical origin, it means that 'The Ould Orange Flute', however Protestant, is also pagan, and pagan of the superstitious kind Reformation Protestantism specifically charged against Catholicism. In a word we would be hard put to determine which sect it extols and which it libels. It mocks Orange pretensions of being 'the ould cause' whence descended the Glorious Revolution, Protestantism, and the Penal Laws against Catholics, whereas in fact the Orange Society, founded in 1795, was the successor and product of all three. It drily indicates the brutality and illegality of Bob Williamson's fate when the 'comment' from the 'boys' sends him into terror-stricken exile, driven from his home and having to choose what he could retain for the hurried journey. Even the narrator himself seems a tad cowardly: beginning with his boast of his part in 'ruction' and his victimisation with the rest of 'us' by Bob's unexpected 'mixed' marriage', he then vanishes. By implication, if anyone ever does convict him of authorship of the song, he will not have incriminated himself by admission of any peace-disturbance or grievous bodily harm in fact or in threat. Above all, the song is funny, and requires everyone, from every sect, to have a little humour.

Although in pleas of persecution by my fellow-Catholics 'The Ould Orange Flute' gets tallied among sectarian songs whose performance is liable to lead to a breach of the peace, common references today are a little uneasy with that classification. There is always the possibility that between the whistles of 'The Protestant Boys' you can hear the Flute laughing, not least because no text of 'Kick the Pope' seems to have survived.

The other major text traditionally associated with Orange self-assertion or bigotry (depending on your taste) is 'The Sash My Father Wore'. Let us accept the text as we get it from an Orange song-book of the mid-1980s, bearing the Imprimatur of David, the future Lord Trimble, some little time before his Nobel Peace Prize winning:

The Sash My Father Wore

Sure I'm an Ulster Orangeman, from Erin's isle I came,
To see my British Brethren all of honour and of fame,
And to tell them of my forefathers who fought in days of
yore,
That I might have the right to wear the sash my father
wore.

CHORUS:
It is old but it is beautiful, and its colours they are fine,
It was worn at Derry, Aughrim, Enniskillen and the Boyne.
My father wore it as a youth in bygone days of yore
An on the twelfth I love to wear the Sash my father wore.

For those brave men who crossed the Boyne have not
fought or died in vain,
Our Unity, Religion, Laws and Freedom to maintain,
If the call should come we'll follow the drum, and cross
that river once more,

That tomorrow's Ulstermen may wear the sash my father
wore.

CHORUS
And when, some day, across the sea to Antrim's shore you
come.
We'll welcome you, in royal style, to the sound of flute and
drum.
And Ulster's hills shall echo still, from Rathlin to Dromore,
As we sing again the loyal strain of the sash my father
wore.

CHORUS.

As usual, the origin is unknown, and in its case there are many
texts. What seems to have been a Music-Hall comic song of the
mid-nineteenth century, 'The Hat My Father Wore', was apparently
the model and inspiration. 'The Sash' itself may not be much older
than 1900. Unlike 'The Ould Orange Flute' it is serious, although
these lines seem innocuous, and presumably would need to be so
to pass muster with proprietors or managers of Glasgow Music-
Halls who (whatever their politics) wanted no danger of rough-
housing, social conflict, charges of bigotry &c endangering their
popularity and their entertainment license. At the same time
the way to make a Music-Hall or pantomime song popular was
to sing it to an already popular air. That Glasgow is the place of
composition, or at least is to be taken as such, the text makes
clear. Dublin in 1912 was still the travel centre of the smaller island,
English passenger ships plying their way there, or to ports farther
south: Scottish passengers might voyage to Dublin, but their Irish
destinations were most likely to bring them in sight of the glens
of Antrim before landing in Belfast or Larne. One popular variant
actually includes a verse beginning

> So here I am in Glasgow town
> To find them girls to see ...

The Music-Halls liked stage 'Business', so an essential prop would
have been the Sash the Singer wore. Now, it is not much noticed
either by Orange votaries or their ethno-religious opponents that

the Orange Sash, worn to the full, can seem startlingly camp to viewers of more cosmopolitan experience than the wearers or their foes. When in their brief and highly tactical moment of unity the two Unionist party leaders David Trimble and the Revd Dr Ian Paisley held hands and danced down the Garvaghy Road in defiance of Government forces of law and order, they looked like a dutiful if neophyte partnership at the Oklahoma Teamsters Drag Ball. Since His Reverence had previously sought to Unite Ireland Against Sodomy, he had only himself to thank for inciting the Devil to put specific ribaldry into spectators' minds. Early twentieth-century Music-Halls were far too fond of Harry Lauder and his kilt to waste much breath macho cat-calling about sartorial feminization, but there may have been enough jeering to advise additional verses expressing the singer's heterosexual preference, chaste, not to say virginal, as his ambitions towards the ladies appears to be. In any case the refrain line of the song carries its own heterosexual credentials since 'my father' by definition had provided the present deponent as evidence of his masculinity. Even so some versions suggest gay solicitation:

> Here am I a loyal Orangemen,
> Just come across the sea,
> For singing and for dancing
> I hope that I'll please thee:
> I can sing and dance with any man
> As I did in days of yore,
> And on the Twelfth I long to wear
> The Sash my Father Wore.

The content of the song is less sectarian than 'The Ould Orange Flute'. A paranoid Papist (of which we still have our plenty)[5], might argue that the 'Flute' incites hatred of Roman Catholic clergy on the charge of Cruelty to Musical Instruments. But, however paranoid, any exact critic of 'The Sash My Father Wore' will find it hard to justify a charge of religious sectarianism. The many opponents of Orangeism who charge their enemies with bigotry in all their works take care to avoid all textual criticism, merely

---

[5] See several contributions to T. M. Devine (ed.), *Scotland's Shame?: Bigotry and Sectarianism in Modern Scotland*, Edinburgh: Mainstream, 2000.

asserting that the singing of 'The Sash' is in itself a sectarian action, and finding enough well-meaning sheep to stampede on the point while keeping at quarantine-length from the actual words. Here the Faculty of Advocates left itself open to suspicion of having been eased into an adverse verdict without sufficient scrutiny of 'The Sash' when censoring Donald Findlay, Q.C., in 1999 for singing it. If the Faculty censored him purely for other songs it should have exonerated him of sectarian intent as regards 'The Sash', and its failure so to do shows a disrespect for public vindication of proof by strict evidence. Mr Findlay behaved like a silly child showing off before less articulate bullies, but the Faculty presumably knows that justice must not only be done, but should be seen to be done, and on 'The Sash' it should have found for Mr Findlay, however much it might dislike him. Mr Findlay, on his side, might prefer to be thought sectarian rather than innocuous, lest the big boys laugh at him, but that is surely his problem rather than the Faculty's. (There is nothing new in having to establish innocence in the teeth of the accused, and Mr Findlay probably sings with his teeth.)

To subject 'The Sash' to the scholarship from which the Faculty of Advocates apparently shrank, its most obvious hallmark would seem to be that it is extremely defensive, and very vague as to whom it is defensive against. We may infer that it fears Catholics, but does not mention them or any euphemism or other evasion for them. We may even more clearly infer that it fears, or is at least hostile to, the Government of the day, but there is no clue to the party in power, or to the party which may be in power in the event of a governmental repression which the song seems to anticipate. The style is pointedly relaxed: if not working-class with knobs on, it has neither the condescension of the upper classes when slumming with a little mob belligerence, nor the mirthless smile of the bourgeousie participating in secret terror at such potential diminution of respectability. (Mr Findlay, QC, tells us that his parents were working-class but, while refusing to ape higher class manners, did not use the working-class classification: this may be more typical than he realises.) The first line of our first, and apparently senior, version seems to trade on the presumed welcome for any Irish song. 'Sure' is an emphatic trade-marking that stage-Irish performance flaunts. 'Erin's Isle' proclaims kinship to Thomas Moore's 'Let Erin Remember'. We have no proof that it was born in Glasgow: it is a standard device for an emigration-conscious ethnic group to simulate an emigrant origin or even emigrant-descended origin for songs patriotic to its culture. Thus Irish-Americans were popularly supposed to rally (and during a pre-battle lull on the American Civil War the Irish on both sides apparently did) to the song 'Deep in Canadian woods we've met /From one bright island flown', chorus 'We'll toast Old Ireland!/ Dear Old Ireland!/'Ireland, boys, hurrah!' – but the author was T. D. Sullivan of Bantry birth and Dublin journalism, and his only American credential a sister-in-law from Louisiana. No doubt he had the Canadian idea from the Canadian Boat Song (famous for its indictment of Highland clearances) whose origins were comparably cisAtlantic and whose poet was probably Walter Scott.[6]

But 'The Sash My Father Wore' almost certainly was an ambassador to Glasgow, as Sullivan's (and Scott's) were to emigrant countrymen in North America. Nominally the 'Ulster Orangeman' is in Glasgow to see his 'British Brethren', i.e. fellow Orangemen, and tell them a set of facts they know perfectly well to the point of extreme tedium (to read rather than listen to a book of standard Orange songs is to sink into an infernal Giudecca frozen in banal repetitiveness). But what he is actually asserting is his Right (and what he hopes to be their support) to wear his father's sash, which means that singer and hearers of first composition assumed that in some way that right was under threat. This right had been successfully asserted in Derry, Aughrim, Enniskillen and the Boyne, according to the innocent songster: if in fact any troops or Williamite civilians had appeared in Orange garb on the walls of Derry or Enniskillen, or in the line of battle at the Boyne or Aughrim, their commanders would at once have had them stripped of such glaring presentation of targets to the enemy's guns. William III himself at the Boyne expressed his utter contempt for the lethal deployment of ideological charismatic symbols when he was informed the reverend and charismatic Walker who had rallied the Protestant defenders of Derry had been slain, and he icily enquired what a clergyman was doing in the firing-line. The French general St Ruth was killed commanding at Aughrim by proving just such

---

[6] The anonymous and illicit editor of the 'Noctes Ambrosiana' in Blackwood's Magazine (July 1829) in which it first appeared was John Gibson Lockhart who had stayed the previous night with Scott, his father-in-law, the indictment of clearances harmonises with that in Guy Mannering, and the poem seems too great for other claimants who in any case had less opportunity of having it published under iron secrecy enforced by an editor who was not supposed to be there.

an identifiable target, sealing the fate of Jacobitism in Ireland. The war aims of the Williamites at the Boyne were stated with less anachronism in 'The Sash' than in 'The Ould Orange Flute': William was famously pledged, by his banner on arriving for what proved his conquest of the British Isles, to maintain the Protestant religion and the liberties of England, which was naturally taken to include the English in Ireland. 'The Sash' was thus correct in saying the 'brave men who crossed the Boyne' (none braver than William himself, rotten with asthma, nearly drowning in the river and carried to the southern side by one of his own soldiers) fought and died 'Our Unity, Religion, Laws, and Freedom to maintain'. 'Unity' might seem a little anachronistic since the Unions of Scotland and England came in 1707 and of Britain and Ireland in 1801, but it was the three kingdoms under the one Protestant crown that applied in 1688, and, for all that the Home Rule crises of 1886-1914 related to existing British Parliament and possible Irish Parliament, it was still the Protestant crown that animated the Orangemen. 'Our Laws ... to maintain' was a little more uncertain, but probably differed from 'Flute' in that it did not mean the Penal Laws against Catholics which were passed against William's wishes, after the Boyne and Aughrim victories, and which pressed down on the Presbyterians in the eighteenth century for all of their common support of William alongside the episcopalians of the Church of Ireland. The Orange order was not always so ecumenical, but by 1886 and Gladstone's first Home Rule Bill the order included many Presbyterians. Ultimately the Laws meant rule from London by whatever means.

Why was 'The Sash' so defensive? It is clear first of all that the singer is aware, and thinks his audience is also aware of past suppressions and bannings of the Order. Sometimes it was banned, sometime it was forbidden to parade, and in 1836 it dissolved itself under London pressure. Although it had flourished under the leadership of catastrophically selfish Royal Dukes (York and Cumberland under their father George III), its catacomb years (as its more clerical members might call them) lingered long in the Orange memory, and despite forming part of the great Unionist alliance beginning in 1886, the Orangemen were proud of their disreputable status until common opposition to Gladstone reduced them to good behaviour where possible. This worked so well that the great Unionist rebellion of 1911-14 mobilised nearly half a million signatories of the Ulster Covenant, pledged to set up their own Provisional Government in the event of Home Rule becoming law. I suspect that 'The Sash' may have been launched in Glasgow with a view to mobilising Scottish support for any such action. Scotland had its Orange lodges, of course, and had drastically split its Liberals on Home Rule in 1886 and afterwards, but the appeal of 'The Sash' was not to the magnates whose agrarian capitalist interests would draw them into Unionist ranks, however drastic the Ulster oratorical rebellion might sound. 'The Sash' drew on Protestant workers and lower middle-class already existing as a unit around Glasgow Rangers and other Football Club supporters. Rangers, like Celtic, were derided in the 1890s as 'the Old Firm', a social cut below gentlemanly Football Clubs. Both of them went political in the early twentieth century to assert themselves against the snobs. As so often happens in lower-class self-articulation, it took the form of hostility to fellow-workers. But before the Great War the Ulster Unionists of the twentieth century could not afford to let their rebellion degenerate into uncontrolled violence. The achievement of Edward Carson, James Craig and their followers in drilling and arming so great an army of civilian supporters stood out in sharp and peaceable contrast to the bloody Belfast Unionist protests against Home Rule in 1886 (when the Liberal championship of Home Rule and the Tory discovery of Ulster electrified the city) and in 1893 (when the Second Home Rule Bill actually passed the House of Commons before its utterly undemocratic defeat in the Lords). Now, in 1911-14, the House of Lords could only interpose a veto for two years and then the Home Rule Bill would be law with Catholic power (though little enough of it) ruling Ireland from Dublin. Yet, at this most perilous of all moments, Carson and Craig turned their mass worker movement into a model of masterly restraint, and 'The Sash' symbolically conscripted the Protestant Scots workers, especially those of Ulster stock, to pledge support without a word threatening the peace of the day, only demanding the right to wear the paternal sash. There might be an indication that 'my father' had worn the Sash in the affrays of 1886 and 1893 but, in fact, the Orangemen had not dressed for rioting (and if they had, the Sash would hardly have been sartorially *comme il faut* when it reached the singer). The song promises to 'cross that river' once more if the drum so ordained, which clearly it would not, since the Boyne was now in the heartland of Catholic Ireland. In fact, for the 'welcome' offered to the Scots, should they come 'some day', their hosts are spoken for from Rathlin Island (northeast of Ireland, where Robert Bruce saw his spider) to Dromore (where in some versions the singer originated, rhyming conveniently as it does with 'wore'): it almost seems as though the Orangemen are only sure of holding Ulster east of the Bann river. As 'Flute' made clear, mid-Ulster was much more debatable land (although urban immigration had built up a strong Catholic ghetto in West Belfast, all the better for city riots).

The one line with a hint of Armageddon was that very expression of readiness to 'cross that river once more'. Ulster Protestants accustomed to evangelical preachment would have automatically thought of the Biblical river Jordan in such a context. And the air was foetid with unspoken apocalypticism. Ultimately, there emerged a truly sectarian call to arms as poem rather than song, Rudyard Kipling's 'The Covenant', later retitled 'Ulster 1912', actually published in the Carsonite *Covenanter* on 20 May 1914, a few weeks before the twice-vetoed Third Home Rule Bill would become law (it did, but the advent of World War I made it a dead letter and the ultimate outcome took more extreme and bloody forms):

> The dark eleventh hour
> Draws on and sees us sold
> To every evil power
> We fought against of old.
> Rebellion, rapine, hate,
> Oppression, wrong and greed
> Are loosed to rule our fate,
> By England's act and deed.
>
> The faith in which we stand,
> The laws we made and guard –
> Our honour, lives, and land –
> Are given for reward
> To Murder done by night,
> To Treason taught by day,
> To folly, sloth, and spite,
> And we are thrust away.
>
> The blood our father spilt,
> Our love, our toils, our pains,
> Are counted us for guilt,

And only bind our chains.
Before an Empire's eyes
The traitor claims his price.
What need of further lies?
We are the sacrifice.

We asked no more than leave
To reap where we had sown,
Through good and ill to cleave
To our own flag and throne.
Now England's shot and steel
Beneath that flag must show
How loyal hearts should kneel
To England's oldest foe.

We know the wars prepared
On every peaceful home,
We know the hells declared
For such as serve not Rome –
The terror, threats, and dread
In market, hearth, and field –
We know, when all is said,
We perish if we yield.

Believe, we dare not boast,
Believe, we do not fear –
We stand to pay the cost
In all that men hold dear.
What answer from the North?
One Law, one Land, one Throne.
If England drive us forth
We shall not fall alone![7]

A few days later he went down to Tunbridge Wells and formally committed treason by instructing the public to resist the Third Home Rule Bill, if enacted, by force if necessary. The only other major creative artist in Britain to identify himself with the signers of the Ulster Covenant and espouse their promise of treason was the Roman Catholic composer Sir Edward Elgar.

---

[7] Rudyard Kipling, *Collected Poems*, London: Wordsworth, 1994, p.243-44.

Notwithstanding Elgar, nobody seems to have put 'Ulster 1912' to music other than its own muted ominous tone. But it was intended for song without music, and was deliberately inflammatory with effect when the Bill became law and Carson gave the signal (to this day nobody can be sure if he would have done). It is a work of genius, all the more because it seethes with deliberate and despicable falsehoods which the poet knew perfectly well were false. It deliberately prophesied, and sought to persuade its Ulster Protestant audience to believe, that Roman Catholicism would extirpate them in the event of Home Rule. Allowance might be made if Kipling believed this. He did not. The previous December he had written to H. A. Gwynne, editor of the *Morning Post*, of 'the South [i.e. the Irish Catholics] playing a game it has not got its heart in', which was true enough: the old Irish Parliamentary Party had become very Anglophile (as some would prove by being killed for the UK), give or take a few traditionalist noises, and the demand for Home Rule was practically formulaic, but no less essential under party political self-definition. The poem went all the way with treason. His letter to Gwynne asked, 'Does it occur to you that a betrayed Ulster will repeat 1688 in the shape of a direct appeal to Germany?' The poem's last line spoke of the Ulster folk not being 'alone', which obviously meant the Tory party under Andrew Bonar Law, also complicit in treason, but what he told Gwynne indicates he thought it might include Germany (and on 24 April the first instalment of German aid arrived at Larne in the shape of guns purchased for the Provisional Government of Unionist Ulster).

We have noticed the artistic and diplomatic limits on sectarian song in the 'Flute' and 'The Sash' but, with due respect to those considerations, neither song seems either anti-Catholic or by an author seriously hostile to Catholicism. The Inquisition is merely funny to the author of the 'Flute' and appears to be irrelevant to the author of 'The Sash'. Kipling for purely inflammatory reasons summons up its ghost, implying that Dante's *Inferno* was managed by the Roman ecclesiastic authorities (most of whom were probably livid at the ease and pleasure with which Dante consigned so many Popes to Hell). And Kipling was not anti-Catholic. What was probably his greatest novel, *Kim*, has an eponymous Irish Catholic boy-hero whose destiny is affected beneficially by a Catholic priest: Kim's own devotion to his *guru* shows that Kipling understood the appeal of clerical mysticism to some Catholic boys better than almost any other writer, however Hindu the *guru*. Kipling's famous 'Soldiers Three' are Irish, Yorkshire, and Cockney, with the Irish Catholic the supreme star of the three. Kipling's poem 'Our Lady of the Sackcloth' captures the act of worship at Catholic consecration in the Mass deepened by Marian iconography, to the grief of a priest sundered from it:

> Never again at the Offering
> When the Wine and the Blood are one!
> Oh, never the picture of Mary
> Watching him honour her Son![8]

How account for 'Ulster 1912', with its supreme emotive demand for sectarian war by likening Unionist Ulster to the Supreme Martyr Himself, Jesus Christ, notably in quoting Caiaphas's 'What need of further witnesses?' when his chosen perjurers had failed him and Jesus therefore gave him the testimony to impugn?

Kipling loved Ireland, Protestant and Catholic, loved it so much that he went berserk at the thought of its being sundered from England. He loved it within a sense of confident fellowship, very different from the devotion he pushed abjectly towards the superior, contemptuous England which he knew despised him as a colonial, married to an American, descendant of Scots Highlanders and Ulster Protestants. As a boy back from India it was Ireland (as presented by G. C. Beresford, 'McTurk' in *Stalky & Co.*) which befriended him when England (in the shapes of his Baldwin and Burne-Jones cousins) refused to house him and, before deliverance to school and Beresford, he had languished in the clutch of a vindictive English female guardian in what he called the house of desolation. How could he let Ireland go? What else could keep him entertained while serving out his time in English service? For neither the author of 'The Sash' nor that of 'Ulster 1912' sounds any love of England. At the depth of their hatred, Rome is not the real enemy, but rather England in its complacent contempt.

---

[8] R. Kipling, *Collected Poems*, p.535-37.

III

Sectarian songs are ultimately war songs. Among the oldest parts of the Bible are two war songs, those of Moses and his followers after the defeat of Pharaoh by the drowning of his army in the Red Sea (Exodus xv. 1-21), and of Deborah the prophetess on her defeat of Sisera and his death (Judges v). They are not, in the initial instance, songs to induce war, or to be sung as it approaches, intended rather to conserve the memory of success in conflict, to be recalled in future times of crisis. Women are associated with the singing, Miriam the prophetess, sister of Aaron and Moses, using timbrel and dance, Deborah, architect of the victory, telling its story with focus on Jael the wife of Heber the Kenite as she drives a hammer into the sleeping Sisera's brain, and, remarkably, on Sisera's mother complaining at his non-arrival when she was looking forward to his carrying Israeli loot to her, particularly divers colours of needlework. It is a chillingly human motivation, much as one finds in recent folk (not to say sectarian) songs. The ethics are fascinating: Jael is commended for giving Sisera milk when he asked for water, thus ensuring she did not violate the dietary requisites of hostly protection, and 'she brought forth butter in a lordly dish'. Touches like that bring home songs, singers and hearers of many centuries hence. A time suggested is the twelfth century BC in each case, a century also given credit for the siege and destruction of Troy, if any, whose most ancient detailed version is the *Iliad*, ascribed to Homer who might have lived anywhere in the subsequent four centuries if at all.

But the tradition was strong that the *Iliad* was the work of a poet named Homer, and as such it would seem to have been popularly repeated. Perhaps its most striking quality, from the historian's perspective, is its extraordinary objectivity. Few historians have come close to its achievement in seeing so much sympathetically from the different points of view of the various actors, above all of the embattled city and its besiegers. It may give geographical credibility to the notion that Homer was native to Chios, Smyrna or some other Greek-populated place in Asia Minor, close to the sea and not too far from Troy. He could see his story (if not his audience) from all sides. So the war-poem or war-song did not have merely to be a yell of elation requiring emulation.

But the finished work (finished at least in the views of almost everyone except its author) to appropriate most from the *Iliad* and its supposed fellow-Homeric Odyssey, Virgil's *Aeneid* (composed two decades before Christ) used the mythical war to assert Roman identity and with it an assumption of Roman superiority to all other peoples. It might be said that this is implicit in the song of Miriam if not in that of Deborah, but the *Aeneid* is no brief hymn of thanks for recitation on festive or crisis occasions; it is an empire's *raison d'être*, and it is more confident of future national success than either Miriam or Deborah, aware as they are that God must not be taken for granted. As such it became the pattern and the paradigm for most national myths in song of whatever length. Composed in an age of probably less religious fidelity than Homer's, it made far more of divine descent for Rome's Julian Emperors. For example, Sarpedon son of Zeus and Achilles son of Thetis are killed in the *Iliad*, however regretted by their divine parents, but Aeneas son of Venus survives war, voyage, and more war in the *Aeneid*. Homer's most conspicuous survivors of the long voyage home and the perils of home itself are Odysseus and Menelaus, neither of divine origin. Sectarian song-singing assumes God is on our side.

Most primitive civilisations had gods to whom they prayed for victory in time of war, and when Christianity was adopted in the Roman Empire and thereafter, cults of local saints were pressed into service, if not Jesus Christ himself: Constantine was claimed as having received promise of divine assistance enabling him to become master of Rome in 312, although he was not baptised a Christian until near his death, 25 years later. The ensuing millennium would see many cases of local gods having been evidently recycled as local Christian saints, continually conscripted for battle against other Christian saints aiding their votaries. Sometimes local saints had been annexed from far away, as with St George for England and St Andrew for Scotland. Armies on the move or their masters might also invoke heroes too warlike to have won canonisation, however honorary: the French troops led at the battle of Hastings by Duke William of Normandy were preceded by a minstrel boy singing of the heroic deaths of Roland and Oliver against the Moors (actually the Basques) nearly three hundred years earlier. It is significant that this song, intended to inspire troops for victory, should have told a story of defeat. We do not know the version of the legend which was sung at Hastings (or Senlac) in 1066, but we can be sure Roland and Oliver were killed in it. The inspiration was therefore the knowledge that French soldiers of courage had died in a French cause: that Roland and Oliver had probably few soldiers of Scandinavian origin (except perhaps Ogier the Dane) was apparently of no account to the Normans under William. Nor was the song's being of a French defeat: what was important was that it spoke of French courage, Christian courage, regardless of its outcome or of the ethno-religious composition of the English enemy. The minstrel, known only as Taillefer, won permission from William to lead the army with his *Chanson* and in some accounts was credited with throwing his sword into pretty little acrobatics and catching it with prompt lethal results for the opposing forces, but these ultimately killed him, despite William's forces by now moving well forward. What he sang, if it was like the version of the *Chanson* we now have, turned on a cry more than a song, rallying Roland's doomed troops. In the aged Young Irelander John O'Hagan's translation in the 1880s:

Then from the Franks resounded high –
'*Montjoie!*' Whoever had heard that cry
Would hold remembrance of chivalry.
Then they ride – how proudly, o God, they ride!
With rowles dashed in the horses' side.
Fearless, too, are their paynim foes.
Frank and Saracen, thus they close.

An Irish interest in the conquest of England may not have been limited to O'Hagan, It may have extended to earlier study of the French original by Thomas Moore who certainly produced something very like Taillefer in his famous song written about 1812:

The Minstrel boy to the war has gone
  In the ranks of death you'll find him!
His father's sword he has girded on
  And his wild harp slung behind him.
'Land of Song', cried the Warrior Bard,
  'Tho' all the world betrays thee,
One sword at least thy rights shall guard,
  One single harp shall praise thee!

The Minstrel fell, but the foeman's chain
   Could not bring that proud soul under!
The harp he lov'd never spoke again,
   For he tore its chords asunder,
And said, 'No chain shall sully thee,
   Thou soul of love and bravery,
Thy strings were made for the pure and free,
   They shall never sound in slavery!'

It is a little rough on the Saxon who, after all, would pass into servitude as a result of the inspiration given to the conquerors by Taillefer, and who would be taken by anyone hearing Moore's song as the 'foeman' whose 'slavery' forced the dying minstrel to silence his own harp. It is also curiously appropriate to 'The Ould Orange Flute' since there again the instrument becomes the symbol of the spirit of freedom against its destructive enemies. Once again the heartwarming courage from one vantage-point becomes the repository of bigotry from the other, Basque or Frank, Saxon or Norman, English or Irish, Protestant or Catholic, with a good deal of art and wit expended *en route*. To complicate the story further Moore, however much inspired by Taillefer, *Montjoie*, Roland &c, would have been meditating on Ireland in 1798, and his minstrel could be Catholic, going to the war in Wexford (or Wicklow or Carlow or Kildare), or Presbyterian, going to the war in Antrim or in Down, or even Church of Ireland, going to the war in Dublin, like Moore's friend Robert Emmet in 1803, to end in a ghastly and bloody fiasco but with a noble speech on which to die, as bloodstirring as the minstrel's if somewhat less succinct.

Sectarian songs are born of defeat, if they are any good: doubtless there are exceptions. But if they inspire victory or renew old convictions, their real strength comes from being well-greased with the bitterness of failure. They are also likely to be anachronistic: their force comes from a well-chewed sorrow, a cold hope of revenge. Yet when the sect becomes a nation, and the nation becomes a country, its song-sheets of identity have to sustain enough dignity and permanence to make a national anthem. It means that victors have to undertake some self-censorship. One song which was not a national anthem but was greatly in sympathy with the existing one had to censor itself so that it might be played on appropriate occasions: 'The British Grenadiers'. It became a popular song in the 1790s and 1800s, against Revolutionary and Napoleonic France. But it first saw service in the immediate aftermath of Culloden a half-century earlier:

> Some talk of Alexander,
> And some of Hercules,
> Of Hector and Lysander,
> And such great men as these:
> But of all the world's great heroes
> There's none that can compeer
> To the Gallant Duke of Cumberland
> And the British Grenadier!

The song was disappeared during the Seven Years War and was only allowed to resurface shorn of the Butcher Cumberland, ignominiously bowdlerised by

> With a Tow-row-row-row-row-row-row-row-row-row
> To the British Grenadier!

This was eighteenth-century sectarian song much as were the anti-Scottish verses of the actual National Anthem ('God Save the King'), subsequently dropped. The boasting of the superiority of the Butcher over classical heroes had some impudence, quite apart from its wallowing in his butcheries: apart from the war crimes of Alexander, the infanticides of Hercules, the blood thirst of Hector and the ruthlessness of Lysander, the eighteenth century itself had military commanders fully the equal of the victor of Culloden (also the vanquished of Fontenoy) as far as massacring a defeated and defenceless army was concerned. But there is some charm in the thought that the apotheosis of Cumberland would give way within three decades of his death to deletion in favour of animal yowls. In their hunger for more bodies to garnish battlefields, the new warlords willingly jettisoned the old, as Byron observed in starting *Don Juan's* First Canto.

   The USA had to make comparable extermination of once-popular sectarianism, as embodied in its 'Star-spangled Banner'. No national anthem can have been born in more crucial circumstances. Francis Scott Key of Maryland sat, a temporary prisoner, in a British man-of-war in September 1814, having been told that Fort McHenry was expected to yield to the UK forces that night, which would mean that Baltimore must fall, and the USA would be cut in two, to end the war of 1812 either reconquered by Britain or fragmented and quivering into nonentity. Key's one clue to the night's fortunes was what could be seen of the US flag which in fact was still flying when dawn came. The poem, apparently written or at least drafted during this ordeal in waiting, recorded the survival of flag, fort and city and thence of country, in the second verse. There followed a vengeful third, for the war had many enemies, some of whom thought of return to their old English masters:

> And where is that band, who so vauntingly swore,
>   That the havoc of war, and the battle's confusion
> A home and a country, shall leave us no more?
>   Their blood has washed out their foul footsteps' pollution!
>   No refuge could save the hireling and slave
>   From the terror of flight or the gloom of the
>   grave,
>   And the star-spangled banner in triumph doth wave
> O'er the Land of the Free, and the Home of the Brave.

The verse is prophecy, reasonably so once the city was saved, but what is slightly uncertain is against whom the doom is pronounced. Most probably its immediate designation would be the British forces, one of whom guarding Key had informed him the previous evening how the USA was sure of defeat since the fort was about to fall. The survival of the fort had meant some measure of British defeat and hence doom could be pronounced on at least some of the attackers. But as the verse continues, its victims seem more likely to be the Americans dreaming of defection in southern New England. This was sectarianism literally with a vengeance. The verse was discarded when US-UK relations became really cordial, which was not until about 85 years later, and at that point it was given out that the verse was offensive to the British. That it also revealed the depth of divisions in the USA itself was officially ignored, but clearly was not something desirable for raucous recollection: it was bad enough that Southern disaffection had become so notorious in the mid-century without notice of early Northern disloyalty being kept before the eyes of the world. It was without the third verse that the song became the national anthem in 1931 (with its present name in place of the original 'Defense of Fort McHenry').

The trouble about National Anthems having started out as Sectarian Songs is that they may have to be amended as well as suffer deletion when later stages of history persuade a country's rulers that they want their history to have been different. The French were able to do it when their 'Marseillaise' was in the process of being born: it was originally begun by cadet supporters of the menaced and indeed doomed Louis XVI and then hi-jacked by revolutionaries whose several successive stages then hi-jacked each one from the previous owner. The Germans were stripped of the first verse of their *'Deutschland Über Alles'* after 1945. What one generation meant may not be what a later generation thinks it meant. The Scots not being an independent nation yet, their national anthem is still a question of taste, but two favourites – 'Scots Wha Hae' and 'The Flower o' Scotland' – both recall the Battle of Bannockburn in 1314, Robert Bruce defeating King Edward of England. But how many people hear either of those songs or sing them under the vague impression that the Edward defied in the song is the Hammer of the Scots, Edward I who reigned from 1273 to 1307? That is certainly a suitable national ogre against whom to rally resistance. His much less effective son, Edward II, ultimately dethroned and disgustingly murdered by his wife, is a poorer choice of tyrant for national myth. Another form of royal ambiguity arose from the very succession dispute which fuelled modern ethno-religious sectarianism, viz. which King is God called on to save? 'God Save the King' itself is separately claimed as originally written for the Stuarts and for the Hanoverians. In any case, the problem of the formula itself was ably summed up by a sardonic Jacobite:

God save the king, I mean, the Faith's Defender.
God bless – no harm in blessing – the Pretender.
But who Pretender is, and who is King,
God bless us all, that's quite another thing!

The honours would seem to go to George III, if Sir Walter Scott was right in his story that, on hearing his cousin Prince Charles Edward was secretly in London soon after George's accession in 1760, the King sent him a message 'The Elector of Hanover presents his compliments to the Chevalier de St Georges'. But few of his supporters would have thanked him for it.

IV

We worry about sectarian songs in Scotland, and party leaders complain that other party leaders have not done enough about it, or have done the wrong thing. But, while the topic has its international and historical relevance, it is curious how little attention has been paid to the original singing contest in Scottish sectarianism. Scottish religion has been more popular than most, whether Catholic or Protestant, but that was not the original meaning of singing sectarianism. We turn back to Clan times where ancient feuds and their modern cultivation devastated much of Scotland, whether Highland, Island, Lowland, or Borders.

The role of the clan bard was vital: he had to affirm clan identity by asserting historical enmity with one clan or more. As the historian Thomas Babington Macaulay, son of a Gaelic-speaking Scot, remarked, the important question in Scottish politics was not, who shall be king?, but what side is MacCallum More (the head Campbell) on? Macdonalds would be on the other side; Macaulays would follow Campbells. Macaulay has useful things to tell us, since in his half Highland identity he seems to have seen himself as a latter-day bard; though not so visible as such to English eyes. He occasionally forgot himself when writing his *History of England* and referred to the Campbells as 'Clan Diarmid', which was good manners from a bard of a subordinate clan but must have puzzled many English. (Diarmuid was the Achilles-like figure of old Fenian legend from whom the Campbells were supposedly descended.) The English seemed too successful to make much of a business of sectarian songs. Clearly, the Scots had a long history of them and the wars they exacerbated, and Macaulay himself sought to create some innocuous songs for the English to enjoy in *The Lays of Ancient Rome*, imaginary bardic narratives supposedly from prehistoric times commemorating even more imaginary events. He was careful to make them songs of festive or commemorative rejoicing, in the case of the first two, 'Horatius' and 'The Battle of Lake Regillus', describing Roman success in repelling Etruscan and Latin attempts to restore the ousted Tarquin monarch but, in both, Etruscans and Latins are handled with respect and even some admiration, with anger evident only against the exiled King and his rapist son Sextus (even his younger son Titus has a minor heroic role). That was consistent with Homeric, and even Virgilian, practice. The last two

Lays were more pragmatic. 'Virginia' was a Plebeian song for use against a Patrician enemy in Roman elections by recalling crimes of his grandfather, and Macaulay's inspirations for that were the Irish Catholics before emancipation in 1829, when they were building up a great pressure group in non-violent agitation under Daniel O'Connell. The last Lay, 'The Prophecy of Capys', was much more exultant and ethnophobe, the Romans having supposedly just defeated the Tarentines in the South and their Greek ally Pyrrhus king of Epirus and his elephants. Whether Macaulay realised it or not he, even more than Capys, was prophesying that Britain would sustain her imperial adventures on highly sectarian songs, pride and greed replacing anger as motivation. Naturally those people they conquered had sectarian songs of their own with which among themselves to curse their conquerors, and conquered Celtic peoples had already composed many.

'Virginia' suggests that Macaulay knew of the existence of such songs among the dispossessed Gaelic Irish, and it is interesting that the Chinese term 'foreign devils' for the Europeans who thrust unequal treaties on them is exactly the same as that employed by Irish Gaelic poets to describe their Protestant English conquerors who have driven them off the best Irish land. Gaelic poetry reflected the dispossessed eighteenth century poets who saw their whole bardic order driven into mendicancy and the chieftains who had patronised them now exiled abroad, and their imprecations on their malefactors would make the most atrocious fan mouthing curses in support of Glasgow Rangers sound like a sucking-dove. Sean Clárach MacDomhnaill's instructions to the devil as to how to treat the soul of the late Colonel Dawson, or Aodhagán Ó Rathaille's exultation at the accidental death of a Protestant clergyman's son are but two of the hymns marinated in vindictiveness, and their two bards were amongst the finest Gaelic poets of the early eighteenth century. Modern Irish Catholic nationalist historians, however partisan, usually express admiration for the bravery of the besieged Protestants in Derry against James II and VII in 1689, but the great Gaelic Farewell to Patrick Sarsfield includes the hope that smallpox will descend on the town.

Macaulay was evidently alarmed by Young Ireland imitations of his *Lays* reviving the hatreds of former centuries. When Charles Gavan Duffy editor of the Dublin *Nation* sent him his anthology *The Spirit of the Nation* in May 1845 he replied:

Some of those songs I already know; and I have been much struck by their energy and beauty. Those which I have not yet read possess, I doubt not, similar merit. But I cannot refrain from saying with how much pain the pleasure which I have received from these compositions has been mingled. I would intreat you to consider whether genius be worthily employed in inflaming animosity between two countries, which, from physical causes such as no political revolution can remove, must always be either blessings or curses to each other.[9]

How fully did Macaulay realise that here he followed William Robertson's diatribe in his *History of Scotland* against fancied considerations of honour leading medieval Scottish clans into murderous and incessant feuds? Walter Scott, Robertson's greatest pupil, echoed his master's voice in *Ivanhoe* (where the Jewish hero, Rebecca, denounced male self-destruction in the absurdities of chivalric code) and *The Fair Maid of Perth* (which showed the homicidal effects of clan confrontation as honour stoked homicidal fires). But at least what Robertson and Scott had denounced were evils born of their time. What Macaulay realised was that Gavan Duffy and his fellow-poets in the *Nation* were using their considerable poetic powers artificially to whip up mutual hatreds between Britain and Ireland by giving English verse and voice to the Gaelic hatreds from two centuries earlier. The romantic confections had an attractiveness because so little of the humanity of the day could be heard, and instead historical personnel addressed one another as high nobility, unmoved by any save idealistic considerations. Gavan Duffy's own evocation of the murderous insurrection of 1641 sought to justify sectarian slaughter by Catholic native against Protestant immigrant:

> Joy! joy! the day is come at last, the day of hope and pride,
> And see! our crackling bonfires light old Bann's
>   rejoicing tide,
> And gladsome bell, and bugle-horn from Newry's
>   captured towers,

---

[9] 26 May 1845, T. B. Macaulay, *The Letters of Thomas Babington Macaulay*, Vol. 4, ed. Thomas Pinney, Cambridge University Press, 1977, pp.259-60.

Hark! how they tell the Saxon swine, this land is ours,
    IS OURS!
Glory to God! my eyes have seen the ransomed
    fields of Down
My ears have drunk the joyful news, 'Stout Phelim
    hath his own'.
Oh! may they see and hear no more, oh! may
    they rot to clay,
When they forget to triumph in the conquest of to-day.
Now, now we'll teach the shameless Scot to
    purge his thievish maw,
Now, now the courts may fall to pray, for Justice is the
    Law.
Now shall the Undertaker square, for once,
    his loose accounts.
We'll strike, brave boys, a fair result, from all
    his false amounts.
Come, trample down their robber rule, and smite
    its venal spawn,
Their foreign laws, their foreign Church, their ermine,
    and their lawn;
With all the specious fry of fraud that robbed us of our
    own,
And plant our ancient laws again beneath our lineal throne.
Our standard flies o'er fifty towers, o'er twice
    ten thousand men,
Down have we plucked the pirate Red, never to rise again;
The Green alone shall stream above our native field
    and flood –
The spotless Green, save where its folds are gemmed
    with Saxon blood.
Pity! No, no, you dare not, Priest – not you, our Father,
    dare
Preach to us now that godless creed – the murderers'
    blood to spare;
To spare his blood, while tombless still our slaughtered
    kin implore,
'Graves and revenge' from Gobbin Cliffs and Carrick's
    bloody shore!
Pity! could we 'forget – forgive', if we were clods of clay,

Our martyr'd priests, our banish'd chiefs, our race
   in dark decay,
And worse than all – you know it, Priest – the daughters
   of our land,
With wrongs we blushed to name until the sword
   was in our hand!
Pity! Well, if you needs must whine, let pity have its way,
Pity for all our comrades true, far from our side to-day.
The prison-bound who rot in chains, the faithful dead
   who poured
Their blood neath Temple's lawless axe or Parsons'
   ruffian sword.
&c. &c.

No wonder Macaulay was horrified. It mingled phrases and appositions of his own from the *Lays*, from 'Ivry', from 'The Battle of Naseby', with some of the most vengeful sentiments that ever adorned a Gaelic rhyme, throwing in a somewhat improbable repudiation of Christianity on the ground that the doctrine of forgiving your enemy was 'godless' (it was in fact Christ's). It may have been that Gavan Duffy was trying to vindicate priests during the 1641 massacres by implying they did what they could to abate the persecutions and slaughters. Oliver Cromwell, nine years after 1641, convinced himself and the Roundheads that the priests were the guiltiest of all in the insurgent atrocities, partly because the Catholic Confederation armies were led by Bishop Heber MacMahon of Clogher during the Cromwellian repression. And they had long memories in the diocese of Clogher, whence Gavan Duffy himself had come. But long memories also sang for the Protestant heirs of those settlers who survived the massacres of 1641, notably those pitchforked from Bloody Bridge to drown in 'old Bann's rejoicing tide'. Irish Protestantism, when Episcopalian, came from a victor culture, so that in its sectarian songs the horrors of the Bann in 1641 are subordinated into the commemoration of the Boyne in 1690. But the Boyne, rippling its way through Catholic-owned fields today, has little future relevance for Ulster Protestantism; the Bann, as Drumcree reminds us, has all too much. The River Foyle at Derry has its own memories of the siege of 1689 and its finest romantic evocation was in prose rather than verse, but a prose singing so well that it was subsequently engraved on the city's revered walls and its author was Macaulay in his *History*:

It was the twenty-eight of July. The sun had just set: the evening sermon in the cathedral was over; and the heartbroken congregation had separated; when the sentinels on the tower saw the sails of three vessels coming up the Foyle. Soon there was a stir in the Irish camp. The besiegers were on the alert for miles along both shores. The ships were in extreme peril: for the river was low; and the only navigable channel was very near to the left bank, where the headquarters of the enemy had been fixed, and where the batteries were most numerous. Leake performed his duty with a skill and spirit worthy of his noble profession, exposed his frigate to cover the merchantmen, and used his guns with great effect. At length the little squadron came to the place of peril. Then the *Mountjoy* took the lead, and went right at the boom. The huge barricade cracked and gave way: but the shock was such that the *Mountjoy* rebounded, and stuck in the mud. A yell of triumph rose from the banks: the Irish rushed to their boats, and were preparing to board; but the *Dartmouth* poured on them a well directed broadside, which threw them into disorder. Just then the *Phoenix* dashed at the breach which the *Mountjoy* had made, and was in a moment within the fence. Meanwhile the tide was rising fast. The *Mountjoy* began to move and soon passed through the broken stakes and floating spars. But her brave master was no more. A shot from one of the batteries had struck him; and he died by the most enviable of all deaths, in sight of the city which was his birthplace, which was his home, and which had just been saved by his courage and self-devotion from the most frightful form of destruction.[10]

That was published as part of the second instalment of Macaulay's *History of England*, appearing in 1855 and becoming, like its predecessor volumes of 1848, a prompt bestseller, as Gavan Duffy's *Nation* had been (highest UK periodical sales in the 1840s). Unlike the *Nation*, Macaulay's *History* was pirated in its entirety across the USA, and there can be little doubt that among the enthusiastic writers who devoured it was the poet Walt Whitman, who put it

---

[10] T. B. Macaulay, *The History of England*, Harmondsworth: Penguin Classics, 1979, pp.316-17.

to use when he heard of Lincoln's assassination in the moment of victory in the American Civil War in April 1865. It was characteristic of him to think of the kind of person who would be isolated in grief for the death of Micaiah Browning, master of the *Mountjoy*: he would have pictured a young cabin-boy or midshipman.

> O Captain! my Captain! our fearful trip is done,
> The ship has weathered every rack, the prize
>   we sought is won,
> The port is near, the bells I hear, the people all exulting,
> While follow eyes the steady keel the vessel grim
>   and daring;
>
>> But O heart! heart! heart!
>> O the bleeding drops of red!
>> Where on the deck my Captain lies,
>> Fallen cold and dead.
>
> O Captain! my Captain! rise up and hear the bells;
> Rise up – for you the flag is flung – for you the bugle trills,
> For you bouquets and ribboned wreaths – for you
>   the shores a-crowding,
> For you they call, the swaying mass, their eager
>   faces turning;
>
>> Here Captain! dear father!
>> This arm beneath your head!
>> It is some dream that on the deck,
>> You've fallen cold and dead.
>
> My Captain does not answer, his lips are pale and still,
> My father does not feel my arm, he has no pulse or will,
> The ship is anchored safe and sound, its voyage
>   closed and done,
> From fearful trip the victor ship comes in with object won;
>
>> Exult, O shores, and ring, O bells!
>> But I, with mournful tread,
>> Walk the deck my Captain lies,
>> Fallen cold and dead.[11]

---

[11] Walt Whitman, *Leaves of Grass*, Sioux Falls, SD: NuVision Publications, 2010, p.187.

As Oscar Wilde said, the greatest criticism that can be given a work of art is to make it the creator of another. These songs – for that is what they are – are sectarian songs (although Macaulay managed other very beautiful laments for the defeat of the Irish Catholics and their degradation and exile at the end of the War of the Two Kings). 'O Captain, my Captain' can even claim to have been sectarian for two causes – Irish Protestantism, and American Unionism – for the poem is a silent epitaph for Micaiah Browning as well as for Abraham Lincoln, and would have been resented by the heirs of their enemies in sectarian spirit. Yet for all of the long protracted mutual hatreds in post-1865 America and post-1689 Ireland, those were civil wars. In the words of the Jesuit poet Gerard Manley Hopkins, 'Abel is Cain's brother, and breasts they have sucked, the same' ('The Wreck of the *Deutschland*'). Lincoln and Jefferson Davis, the Confederate President, were both natives of Kentucky. James II and VII was William III's uncle and father-in-law. Louis XIV, James's great ally and William's lifelong foe, was James's first cousin and William's first cousin once removed.

But what becomes of the sectarian song whose parents symbolise the combatants? A. E. Housman's 'The Welsh Marches' captures the horror when the frontier is the bodies of our father and mother, the inheritance descending to a single person:

> High the vanes of Shrewsbury gleam
> Islanded in Severn stream;
> The bridges from the steepled crest
> Cross the water east and west.
>
> The flag of morn in conqueror's state
> Enters at the English gate:
> The vanquished eve, as night prevails,
> Bleeds upon the road to Wales.
>
> Ages since the vanquished bled,
> Round my mother's marriage-bed;
> There the ravens feasted far
> Above the open house of war:
>
> When Severn down to Build was ran
> Coloured with the death of man,
> Couched upon her brother's grave

The Saxon got me on the slave.

The sound of fight is silent long
That began the ancient wrong;
Long the voice of tears is still
That wept of old the endless ill.

In my heart it has not died,
The war that sleeps on Severn side;
They cease not fighting, east and west,
On the marches of my breast.

Here the truceless armies yet
Trample, rolled in blood and sweat,
They kill and kill and never die;
And I think that each is I.

None will part us, none undo
The knot that makes one flesh of two,
Sick with hatred, sick with pain,
Strangling – When shall we be slain?

When shall I be dead and rid
Of the wrong my father did?
How long, how long, till spade and hearse
Put to sleep my mother's curse![12]

That is the one form of sectarian song whose singing no
government needs to outlaw. There is no song of sect that bites
deeper. And its author was a great classical scholar who imagined
Shropshire with no genealogical inheritance from its inhabitants.
The greater the imagination needs to be, the greater the art.

---

[12] A. E. Housman, *Collected Poems*, London: Wordsworth Poetry Library,
1994, p.46.

V

So sectarian songs are the fruit of insufficiently digested history? It could be so, but the examples under recent scrutiny do not seem to be so. Rather, the historical dimension has become threadbare to the point of nudity. Directing our fire (whether from firearm or football-boot) at the alleged supporters of Celtic Glasgow and Glasgow Rangers, their songs (stretching the term to infinity) are not products of Scottish history, in such as I have seen or heard. 'The Sash' and the 'Flute', if employed during a game, in recent times seem to have enjoyed the honorary status of Chinese ancestors, requiring devotion but not being the real basis of physical intervention. To make a good logical connection one would have to say that the singing of a certain sectarian song during a game was clearly the main cause of a subsequent riot, and in certain cases it may be so, but it is much less easy to prove than to do. Were we to give an examination question, it might run: Place in order of probable responsibility for a riot after a Celtic v Rangers game (a) the result, whether win or draw; (b) the referee; (c) gestures, insults or other expressions of contempt and hostility by spectators; (d) the information, conveyed by supposed singing, that the singer's father liked the colour of his cummerbund. (d) seems doomed to the duffer's place on any estimate. But what songs have been recently singled out with attention to their actual contents are not merely insulting but also fraudulent, and ultimately more offensive to the team they allegedly support than to their opponents.

Let us take the repulsive 'Famine Song', leeching on what seems originally to have been a canal song from the early nineteenth century, 'I want to go home':

> I often wonder where they would have been
> If we hadn't taken them in,
> Fed them and washed them,
> Thousands in Glasgow alone.
> From Ireland they came
> Brought us nothing but trouble and shame.
> Well the famine is over.
> Why don't you go home?

It then makes some allusion to rape and incest which for some reason it thinks peculiar to the players and / or supporters of Celtic Glasgow: in reality, there are no frontiers to these horrors, and allusions to them are just as likely to apply to Rangers as to Celtic. It continues:

> You turned on the light
> Fuelled U-boats by night
> That's how you repay us
> It's time to go home.

Now, insofar as any sense at all can be extracted from this, it means that the Rangers players and their supporters are so terrified by the football prowess of Glasgow Celtic that they dare not risk another match against them but want them to go 'home', i.e. to somewhere else. It is the strangest form of support with which any Football Club has ever been inflicted. It is also clear that the singer is complaining that Celtic and its supporters were admitted into the UK during the Great Famine of 1845-52 and remained in Glasgow while simultaneously refuelling Nazi U-boats in Irish ports a century later. They are taken to be immigrants, although most Irish migration to Scotland in modern times happened when Ireland and Glasgow were in the same country, viz. the United Kingdom of Great Britain and Ireland. The Celtic entourage are told they 'brought us nothing but trouble and shame': the one thing we can say they did do was to play a major part in the transformation of Glasgow from a townlet to a megalopolis, so that Glasgow Rangers evidently regard their own city as possessed only of trouble and shame. Historically, the first years of Rangers (from the 1870s) and Celtic (from the 1880s) were passed in mutual goodwill, conscious of the contempt held for both of them by footballers and supporters of more snobbish Clubs. Hostility seems to have sharpened in the Great War, with the myth of Irish-born Catholics stealing the jobs of Protestants at the front. The Irish-born and Irish-descended Catholics served in the UK forces in that war in large numbers but, when the postwar Anglo-Irish conflict broke out in 1919, it became advisable for Great War veterans and their families to keep silent about their service, inviting possible reprisals from the new Sinn Féiners or the new Protestant Action *gauleiters* on the alert for Catholics getting above themselves. It is at this time (1912-22), and not before, that Rangers seem to have associated themselves with Orange Societies and Ulster Protestant traditions in general: Rangers is no more Scottish in its traditions than Celtic, the supporter paraphernalia of both are Irish. In fact Rangers sectarianism followed extensive Ulster Protestant migration to Glasgow.

But Celtic's Irishness is even odder. It likes to flaunt Irish national colours fashionable since 1922, the foundation of the Irish Free State and the end of settlement from non-Ulster Ireland in Scotland (apart from a few trickles, such as myself). The new world of the Irish Free State and its successor entities (Éire, and the Republic of Ireland) boasted new national athletics in the Gaelic Athletic Association which 'banned' any person going to 'foreign' games such as that played by Glasgow Celtic. In other words, Celtic liked to wave the Irish tricolour, flag of an Ireland which regarded players and supporters of Glasgow Celtic as athletically non-persons. They would sing the revoltingly militaristic Irish national anthem whose lines spoke a refusal of asylum to despots or slaves, into either of which categories the G.A.A. consigned Celtic and its followers. Living in this condition of noisy non-existence, Celtic supporters took up uglier causes such as the IRA and its Brighton bombings with nauseating songs claiming that murders of civilians were only a fair retribution for voter discrimination in Lisnaskea. The object would seem to have been to lower Glasgow Celtic in a condition of being a Gaelic, Hibernic, and moral untouchable. In a word, for all that they apparently warred on one another, Celtic and Rangers were very much the same thing: people who were terrified to admit that they and all they stood for were dead, doomed, and meaningless in either Scotland or Ireland, apart from the antics of indecently rich footballers, few of whom had any historic affiliation other than nominal with the yahoos disporting themselves supposedly in their honour. Neither could be told to go home: spiritually, whatever they claimed, they had no homes to go to. Irish nationalists could claim Scottish parentage, since Burns and Scott set out the form romantic Irish nationalism might take when it had forgotten its Gaelic. Ulster Unionism could also claim Scottish links. But neither cause exist by feeding solely on an artificial synthetic diet.

Sectarianism contained much that was despicable and indeed destructive of its own beliefs. But it did know what it stood for, at least to some degree. What survives today is a foul mutation, an abortion whose time has gone. Probably the best means of dealing with Celtic and Rangers mobs is to ban the Irish tricolour and related songs on the grounds that their use in football histrionics constitute insults to a friendly power, and to ban the Union Jack and related songs on the grounds that they constitute attempts to bring into odium, hatred, ridicule, and contempt the national regalia of the UK and are thus breaches of the Queen's Peace, her crown and dignity. They might also fine all the footballers, since it is increasingly evident that they encourage fan macho histrionics. All money collected from fines could be put to use in maintaining athletic training centres to further UK success at the Olympic Games in the future. Oh, and by the way, it is UK: Northern Ireland Protestants and Catholics have been justly enraged by this 'Team GB' stuff, whose failure to include Northern Ireland in its self-congratulation must have aided disaffection during the riot season. Just to be fair all round, let us fine Lord Coe as well.

'At Hame Wi' Freedom':
The Politics of Hamish Henderson

Eberhard Bort

So came all ye at hame wi' Freedom
Never heed whit the hoodies croak for doom.[1]

Tom Nairn felt very sorry that Hamish Henderson could not see the Meadows in Edinburgh teeming with protesters in July 2005, when a huge number of people gathered there to 'Make Poverty History'.[2] Surely, he would have been on the march for independence which led from the Meadows to Princes Street Gardens, on 29 September 2012. Or would he? It is of course a hypothetical question – more than ten years after his death in 2002. But an intriguing one. After all, he died as a card-carrying member not of the SNP, nor the Scottish Socialist Party, but of Scottish Labour, which he had – 'perhaps surprisingly for some', as Steve Byrne put it[3] – joined around the time of the 1997 General Election victory.

How does that square with all those claims about Henderson being a 'republican socialist'[4] and 'the most dangerous left-wing nationalist in Scottish politics'?[5] Did he change his views? Perhaps mellow in old age?

---

[1] Hamish Henderson, 'The Freedom Come-All-Ye', *Collected Poems and Songs*, edited by Raymond Ross, Edinburgh: Curly Snake Publications, 2000, p.143.

[2] Tom Nairn, 'Democratic Warming', *London Review of Books*, 4 August 2005, p.19.

[3] See Steve Byrne, 'Working on the Hamish Henderson Papers', in E Bort (ed.), *'Tis Sixty Years Since: The 1951 Edinburgh People's Festival Ceilidh and the Scottish Folk Revival*, Ochtertyre: Grace Note Publications, 2011, p.179.

[4] Murray Ritchie in the *Glasgow Herald*, 29 June 1987 – quoted in Tim Neat, *Hamish Henderson: A Biography, Vol.II: Poetry Becomes People*, Edinburgh: Birlinn, 2009, p.8.

[5] Tim Neat, *Hamish Henderson*, Vol.II, p.8.

Putting Gramsci into Practice

Before the war, when studying French and German at Cambridge, Hamish Henderson became a communist, influenced by Cambridge Marxists E P Thompson and Raymond Williams, but his communism was coloured by his Episcopaleanism and a very strong cultural nationalism. He began championing Hugh MacDiarmid's and Sorley MacLean's poetry. In Germany, in 1939, he came face to face with 'the Nazi cult of Hitler.'[6] He helped a network set up by a Quaker organisation wich helped Jews to escape Nazi Germany. When the war came, he enlisted to fight against fascism.

The war in the African desert inspired his *Elegies for the Dead in Cyrenaica* (1948), but it was the camaraderie among the soldiers which sharpened his sense of community. In Italy, fighting side by side with the partisans, he was introduced to the work of Antonio Gramsci, 'probably the most original communist thinker of the 20th century in Western Europe', according to the late Eric Hobsbawm:[7]

> Hamish was the first translator of Gramsci's prison works into English but in many ways he was also the first to put Gramsci's prison writings into practice. Gramsci's philosophy fitted very well with Hamish's own developing views of a more humanistic socialism rooted deeply within and developing organically from Scottish/Celtic working class community and culture.[8]

There is some confusion as to whether Henderson ever joined the Communist Party – although he regularly worked with Communists and in Communist-led organisations, for example as secretary to the Scottish USSR Friendship Society, as well as with Hugh MacDiarmid and Sorley MacLean. He also wrote regularly for the *Daily Worker*. While Bill Scott maintains that Hamish 'never actually joined the Communist Party,'[9] Dick Gaughan claims that he

---

[6] Angus Calder, 'Hamish Henderson', *The Independent*, 12 March 2002.

[7] Quoted in Hamish Henderson, 'Introduction to *Prison Letters* of Antonio Gramsci', *Alias MacAlias*, pp.345-64; p.346.

[8] Bill Scott, 'Hamish Henderson's Torch of Freedom', *Frontline*, Vol.2, issue 11, January 2010.

[9] *Ibid.*

'left the party over Hungary in '56.'[10] And Tim Neat wrote in 2002
that Hamish had been ' in turn a member of the Communist party,
the Labour party and the Scottish Labour party.'[11] Maybe Angus
Calder got it right by describing as 'small c communism' what
provided Hamish 'with his perspective on human life.'[12] Alex Wood
came to the conclusion that Hamish 'may in his youth have been a
communist: he was never a Marxist.'[13]

He was certainly not a Marxist theoretician. Corey Gibson
has shown that his interest in Gramsci was deeply personal and
affectionate – he felt an affinity between his Scots origin and
Gramsci's Sardinian roots, picking up on the similarities in the
language situation, and the existence in the shadow of a much
larger and more powerful neighbour – Sardinia being, in Chris
Harvie's words, 'the Italian equivalent of the Highlands'.[14] He
was less interested in the political theory – Gramscian terms like
'cultural hegemony' or 'traditional and organic intellectuals' are,
Gibson writes, 'conspicuous in their absence.'[15] What Henderson
found fascinating were the remarks Gramsci made about folk
culture in the *Prison Notebooks*:

> In Gramscian terms, 'folklore', as a world-view, is necessarily
> 'subaltern' rather than 'hegemonic'; existing in opposition

[10] Dick Gaughan, 'Hamish Henderson: A Personal Appreciation', *The Herald*, 14 March 2002.

[11] Timothy Neat, 'The poetic genius of war', *The Sunday Times*, 10 November 2002. In Vol. I of his biography, five years later, Tim Neat states: 'there is no documentary evidence that he ever actually joined the Communist Party of Great Britain' (p.263), although he worked very closely with its Cultural Committee in Scotland.

[12] Angus Calder, 'Introduction', in Hamish Henderson, *Alias MacAlias: Writings on Songs, Folk and Literature*, edited by Alec Finlay, Edinburgh: Polygon, 2004, p.xiii.

[13] Alex Wood, 'Scotland's folk hero: Hamish Henderson', *Scottish Review*, 7 January 2010.

[14] Christopher Harvie, *Scotland and Nationalism: Scottish Society and Politics 1707 to the Present*, London: Routledge, (fourth ed.) 2004, p.7.

[15] Corey Gibson, '"Gramsci in Action": Antonio Gramsci and Hamish Henderson's Folk Revivalism', in E Bort (ed.), *Borne on the Carrying Stream: The Legacy of Hamish Henderson*, Ochtertyre: Grace Note Publications, 2010, pp. 239-56; p.240.

to "official" conceptions of the world' and offering a counterpoint of perpetual resistance, due to its very existence.[16]

Henderson was aware of the Janus-faced nature of folk culture, as emphasised by Gramsci – forward- and backward-looking. For him, the burgeoning Scottish Folk Revival became a conscious translation into practice of Gramsci's theories, a constant emphasis of 'the possibilities of a political utilisation of folklore – the fostering of an *alternative* to official bourgeois culture, seeking out the positive "progressive" aspects of folk culture.'[17]

Causes and Campaigns

Throughout his life, particularly after returning from the war, Hamish Henderson took up causes and engaged in political campaigns, from writing the 'Ballad of the Men of Knoydart' (1948) in support of the Highland crofters and radical land reform to the anti-Poll Tax protests of the late 1980s.

His stint in Belfast as a WEA (Workers Education Association) secretary in the late 1940s reinforced his anti-sectarianism; he was, as it were, inoculated against it – he had, as he wrote retrospectively in 1974 about his time in Northern Ireland, 'assembled a fair-sized collection of sectarian publications originating on both sides of the religious divide.'[18] He also strove to bridge other divides – Highland and Lowland, urban and rural workers, Irish and Scots, as superbly demonstrated in his 'John MacLean March' (1948), written at the very beginning of his stay in Belfast for the twenty-fifth anniversary of MacLean's death in Glasgow:

> Hi, Neil whaur's your hadarums, ye big Hielan teuchter?
> Get your pipes, mate, an' march at the heid o' the clan.
> Hullo Pat Malone, sure I knew you'd be here son:
> The red and the green, lad, we'll wear side by side.

---

[16] *Ibid.*, p.244.

[17] Hamish Henderson, 'Introduction to *Prison Letters* of Antonio Gramsci', *Alias MacAlias*, p.356.

[18] Hamish Henderson, *The Armstrong Nose*, p.216.

Gorbals is his the day, and Glasgie belongs tae him:
Ay, great John MacLean's comin' hame tae the Clyde.[19]

Hamish would speak out against triumphalist Orange marches and against Catholic bigotry.[20]

Hamish attended the first meeting of the Scottish Convention in 1949. Despite his doubts about its efficiency, he gave its plans for the Scottish Covenant, a plebiscite for what he later called 'an exceedingly moderate measure of Home Rule,'[21] his full backing. It achieved over a million signatures, but no concrete results. 'The Labour Government of the day,' Hamish wrote to *Tribune* in 1966, 'had conveniently forgotten the pro-Home Rule opinions of Keir Hardie, James Maxton and other pioneers of the Labour movement.'[22] Tim Neat sums up Hamish's political outlook in the early 1950s:

> He wanted a Scottish Parliament and he wanted Scotland to take the lead in the international pursuit of world peace. He was a socialist with strong communist leanings but he saw socialism not as a form of party government but 'the process' by which Scotland would govern herself, look after her own, and pursue peace and wellbeing in the world.[23]

He campaigned simultaneously against a planned rocket rage on Benbecula and for the release of the black singer Paul Robeson from prison in the US. In the late 1950s, the campaign for nuclear disarmament gained momentum, and Hamish was one of the first to join in by writing campaign songs. It came to a head when the British Government, in 1960, announced that a US submarine base would be established in the Holy Loch, north of Glasgow, where submarines with nuclear Polaris missiles were to be stationed. The protests produced what Morris Blythman called 'the first real singing campaign ever undertaken in Scotland,'[24] culminating in

---

[19] Hamish Henderson, *Collected Poems and Songs*, p.126.

[20] See Hamish Henderson, *The Armstrong Nose*, p.59; p.199, p.216.

[21] *Ibid.*, p.153.

[22] *Ibid.*

[23] Timothy Neat, *Hamish Henderson*, Vol.I, pp.199-200.

[24] Quote in Ewan McVicar, *The Eskimo Republic: Scots Political Song in*

the 1962 Folkways recording *Ding Dong Dollar*, full of agit-prop
adaptations like

> Oh ye cannae spend a dollar when ye're deid
> No ye cannae spend a dollar when ye're deid
> Singing, Ding Dong Dollar, everybody holler
> Ye cannae spend a dollar when ye're deid.[25]

Hamish Henderson did not only write the sleeve notes for the
record, he also contributed its most lasting song: 'The Freedom
Come-All-Ye' (1960). Written in the spring of 1960 for its time –
he dedicated it to 'the Glasgow Peace marchers' against nuclear
weapons – it transcends it. Its imagery of the 'roch' winds of
change, its rejection of military imperialism, of Scotland's historical
involvement in British imperial wars, and its anti-apartheid message
envisage a future of peace, justice and equality, reminiscent of
the final verse of Robert Burns's 'A Man's a Man For A' That'. It is
an anthem of Scottish internationalism, a song, in Duncan Glen's
words, that belongs 'to all time and all people.'[26]

Its final lines, 'And a black boy frae yont Nyanga / Dings the
fell gallows o' the burghers doon,'[27] point towards Hamish's next
major campaign. The Sharpeville Massacre of 1960 had 'brought
the brutality of Apartheid to the consciousness of the world.'[28] In
1963, Nelson Mandela and nineteen fellow members of the African
National Congress (ANC) were captured on 'Rivonia', a farm in
South Africa were they had taken refuge. Impressed by Mandela's
speech from the dock, and outraged by Mandela's imprisonment
on Robben Island, Hamish responded with 'Rivonia' (1964)

> They have sentenced the men of Rivonia
> Rumbala rumbala rumba la
> The comrades of Nelson Mandela
> Rumbala rumbala rumba la

Action, 1951-1999, Linlithgow: Gallus Publications, 2010, p.96.

[25] *Ding Dong Dollar: Anti-Polaris and Scottish Republican Songs*, Folkways
FW 05444/FD 5444 (1962).

[26] Quoted in Timothy Neat, *Hamish Henderson*, Vol.II, p.186.

[27] Hamish Henderson, *Collected Poems and Songs*, p.143.

[28] Timothy Neat, *Hamish Henderson*, Vol.II, p.187.

He is buried alive on an island
Free Mandela Free Mandela
He is buried alive on an island
Free Mandela Free Mandela.[29]

Pete Seeger sang it, it was picked up by the black South African group Atté, and a version of it occupied the No.1 spot in the Tanzanian charts for five months. It was also smuggled into Mandela's prison and, when Mandela eventually came to Glasgow to receive the Freedom of the City, twenty-nine years later, on 9 October 1993, he and Hamish sang 'Rivonia' from the balcony of the City Chambers. Hamish Henderson had never tired in his campaign against the Apartheid regime. In December 1969, when the South African Springboks stopped at Murrayfield on their Rugby Union tour, the Anti-Apartheid campaign demonstrated in solidarity with the ANC's boycott policy, and Hamish not only denounced (in a letter to the *Scotsman*) 'the tacit connivance of a Labour Government,'[30] but threw himself into the midst of what became known as 'the battle of Murrayfield'. He was arrested when, after the 'battle', he went to the police headquarters in the High Street to protest against police brutality. In January 1970, he was fined £30 for 'causing an obstruction outside Edinburgh City Police Station.'[31]

Had the Second World War been fought to allow South African Apartheid to flourish, he asked, and defended international solidarity with the ANC against accusations that 'militant' demonstrations were counter-productive. He reminded those critics of the ill-conceived appeasement of the 1930s and, again in a letter to the *Scotsman*, came up with a beautiful phrase that would make a good epitaph:

Freedom is never, but never, a gift from above; it invariably has to be won anew by its own exercises.[32]

---

[29] Hamish Henderson, *Collected Poems and Songs*, p.150.

[30] Hamish Henderson, *The Armstrong Nose*, p.183.

[31] See Timothy Neat, *Hamish Henderson*, Vol.II, pp.191-94.

[32] Hamish Henderson, *The Armstrong Nose*, p.185-86.

Other campaigns in the early 1970s concerned demonstrations against the 'milk-snatcher' Margaret Thatcher's education policy, support for the Upper Clyde shipbuilders, and forming the Edinburgh Chile Solidarity Committee after the CIA-engineered overthrow of the democratically elected President of Chile, Salvador Allende, in 1973. In 1974, he demonstrated, side by side with John Smith and Gordon Brown, against admission charges to national galleries and museums.[33]

Also in the early 1970s, Hamish Henderson intervened in the sexual liberation debate on behalf of 'personal sexual happiness'. Himself bisexual, he did not like the word 'gay', but castigated the 'hoary misconceptions and prejudices relating to homosexuality' and the 'panic fear of homosexuality ... endemic in puritan patrist societies.[34] While that letter to the *Scotsman* had remained unpublished, a year later, in 1972, he reiterated 'the self-evident truth that the homosexually oriented person has as undeniable a right to personal sexual happiness as anyone else.' This time the paper carried his letter in which he declared the 'dichotomy of "homosexual" and "heterosexual" ... highly artificial,' and noted, citing Marshall Luhan, that the world was rapidly changing, 'and that these changes include a new tolerance for and interest in differentness.'[35] In December 1974, he supported an Edinburgh meeting of the International Gay Rights Congress.[36]

1973/74 saw, at long last, the publication of *The Prison Letters of Antonio Gramsci* (in three consecutive issues of *New Edinburgh Review*). Hamish was, at that time, involved in the preparations for *The Red Paper on Scotland*, to be edited by Gordon Brown who was the Rector of Edinburgh University. Hamish's influence on Brown, as Owen Dudley Edwards shows in his chapter in this volume, must not be underestimated – it shows, for example, in the phrase that he used in a letter to Hamish where he describes *The Red Paper* as 'a speculative document, which attempts to correct the futile dichotomy between nationalism and internationalism.'[37] Eventually, Hamish was prevented by illness from contributing to

---

[33] Timothy Neat, *Hamish Henderson*, Vol.II, p.238.

[34] *Ibid.*, pp.203-04.

[35] *Ibid.*, pp.209-10.

[36] *Ibid.*, p.241.

[37] *Ibid.*, p.247.

The Red Paper, but he was involved in the next step that followed: when the break-away Scottish Labour Party was set up to advocate radical Home Rule in 1976, by the likes of Jim Sillars (since 1970 Labour MP for South Ayrshire), John Robertson (Labour MP for Paisley) and Alex Neil (Labour researcher) and John McAllion, Hamish joined that party at its inaugural meeting and became one of its activists, becoming the chair of the Edinburgh branch. David Ross told Tim Neat:

> It was quite a branch, with the journalists Neal Ascherson and Rory Watson, the political philosopher Tom Nairn and Sorley MacLean all members. Hamish took the whole thing very seriously indeed.[38]

It was short-lived. A row over the association of SLP members with the International Marxist Group led, despite the best efforts of Hamish Henderson, to the party's disintegration. Jim Sillars joined the SNP, was elected an MP again, became deputy convener of the party (and is today one of the arch critics of Alex Salmond inside the SNP); John McAllion joined Labour (and would later become an MP for Dundee East and an MSP, before joining the Scottish Socialist Party in 2006), Alex Neil also joined the SNP, became an MSP in 1999 and is currently Health Secretary at Holyrood. Another SLP veteran, Colin Boyd, would later become Lord Advocate.

As the SLP faded into the void, the next battle was already looming. Maggie Thatcher *ante portas*. But it is surprising that *The Armstrong Nose* contains only one letter each for 1978 and 1979 – one about MacDiarmid's plagiarism with the fine line that 'Plagiarists of genius are the justified sinners of literature,' and the other a letter to Hamish about an issue of *Tocher*.[39] No mention at all of the 1979 referendum!

It was the disappointing outcome of the referendum which helped to topple the Callaghan government at Westminster and opened the doors of No.10 Downing Street to Margaret Thatcher. All Tory promises made by Ted Heath and Alec Douglas-Home about a more advantageous devolution deal for Scotland were reneged on, and the Thatcher government began to impose policies on Scotland, despite having only a minority of Scottish MPs.

---

[38] *Ibid.*, p.248.

[39] Hamish Henderson, *The Armstrong Nose*, pp.233-35.

In the wake of the Falklands War of 1982 – Hamish would later describe it as her 'letting the genie of jingoism out of the bottle'[40] – Hamish Henderson was informed by Downing Street In December 1983 that he was offered an OBE (Order of the British Empire) in the New Year Honours List. He tore up the letter and flushed it down the toilet, but also wrote back to Margaret Thatcher's office that 'in view of her suicidal defence policies' he could not see his way to accepting this honour. In a statement to the media, he expanded his response, saying that he could not 'be bought off by an honour offered by a British government advancing policies that I have spent my life opposing.'[41] A month later, the listeners of BBC Radio Scotland voted him 'Scot of the Year'. And Brian McNeill celebrated the occasion by composing a Strathspey, 'Hamish Henderson's Refusal'.[42] Imagine the horror, had he accepted the OBE in the very year the government would wage its war against the miners. All in all, a perfect vignette to illustrate the 1980s in Scotland.

Five years later, Hamish Henderson was involved in the anti-Poll Tax campaign. He called the tax 'utterly immoral' and 'utterly stupid' and vowed 'to fight this one out to the bitter end.'[43] He backed the Campaign for a Scottish Parliament, singing 'The Freedom Come-All-Ye' in front of 25,000 demonstrators in the Meadows in Edinburgh on 12 December 1992.[44] He was a founder-member and active supporter of 'Democracy for Scotland' and their Vigil at the foot of Calton Hill.[45]

After the resounding Yes-Vote in the referendum of 1997, the first elections for a Scottish Parliament in nearly 300 years were held in May 1999, Many thought that 'The Freedom Come-All-Ye' would have made a great song to inaugurate the Parliament with – but Burns's 'A Man's A Man For A' That' pipped it to the post. Hamish watched the official opening of the Parliament on 1 July 1999 on television, having not been invited among the great and

---

[40] Quoted in Timothy Neat, *Hamish Henderson*, Vol.II, p.349.

[41] Quoted in *ibid*, pp.265-66.

[42] Brian McNeill, *Unstrung Hero*, Temple COMD2017, 1985.

[43] Hamish Henderson, *The Armstrong Nose*, p.288.

[44] See Christopher Harvie, 'Hamish Henderson: The Grand Old Man of Scottish Folk Culture', in E Bort (ed.), *'Tis Sixty Years Since*, p.142.

[45] See Ivor Birnie, 'At the Vigil: Hamish Henderson and the Campaign for a Scottish Parliament', in E Bort (ed.), *'Tis Sixty Years Since*, pp.157-58.

famous to attend in person. But he enjoyed Sheena Wellington's singing of Burns.

Now that the Parliament was safely established, the Vigil, having lasted 1979 days, was ended, and a ceremony was held on Calton Hill on St Andrews Day 1999 to mark the occasion. Hamish attended and, after the singing of 'The Freedom Come-All-Ye', he addressed the congregation:

> Freedom. A few years back it seemed a puff of wind would blow all this out. But today, it is not a question of why but when. I will not live to see it – but I wish you all the very best.[46]

Scotland's Voice

So, had he lived, would he have joined the Scotland Yes campaign? Would he have spoken at the rally in Princes Street Gardens, alongside Alex Salmond, Margo MacDonald and Dennis Canavan? Surely, he would throw his considerable weight behind the independence campaign? Was that not his life's ambition? Well, it is more than likely.

John McAllion would have no doubt, going by his contribution to the Scottish Parliament debate on Hamish Henderson in 2002:

> He struggled for home rule all his life, not as an end in itself, but as a means to his goal of ultimate independence for Scotland, which he always wanted to see.[47]

And Colin Fox of the Scottish Socialist Party introduced the subject of his Hamish Henderson lecture at the 2012 People's Festival (in itself a homage to Hamish) as 'a socialist, an internationalist, and advocate for independence and a modern Scottish republic.'[48]

---

[46] Quoted in Timothy Neat, *Hamish Henderson*, Vol.II, p.354.

[47] John McAllion, Scottish Parliament debate, 27 March 2002, <http://archive.scottish.parliament.uk/business/businessBulletin/bb-02/bb-03-12f.htm>.

[48] Colin Fox, Hamish Henderson Memorial Lecture, Word Power Books, Edinburgh, 17 August 2012.

For many, 'The Freedom Come-All-Ye' seems to urge: Go for independence, be 'at hame wi' freedom, / Never heed whit the hoodies croak for doom.'

> We certainly have had a few hoodies croaking fer [sic] doom recently and blatantly using the media – including the 'impartial' BBC – to spread their propaganda. As I remember the old Scots, a 'hoodie' was someone who was likened to a hoodie craw which was considered to be selfish, opportunistic and unreliable. (One who would raid his neighbour's nest when he was from home.) So Hamish tells us that our attempts to establish our independence will come under verbal attack from the hoodies in our community, and he was not wrong there.[49]

As nuclear disarmament was a constant concern of Hamish Henderson, Andy Anderson certainly has a point in stressing that aspect of the song – after all it was written for that cause in the first place:

> Because it is now clear and indisputable that a 'yes' vote in the Scottish referendum will kill off the weapons of mass murder stored under the mountains between beautiful Loch Lomond and Loch Long, as far as Scotland is concerned. It is now also clear that what is left of 'Britain' after Scotland leaves will be most unlikely to be able to retain a nuclear weapon of mass destruction and to find a "suitable" home for it.
>
> This could finally bring the political class in Scotland, and the rest of the UK, to a realisation that their imperialistic dreams are over and that 'Great Britain' is no longer a 'leading power' in the modern world needing to show its muscle all over the globe to keep the subjugated 'subjects' in order. Just as it kept Scots, Irish, Welsh and English subjects in order for so long.

---

[49] Andy Anderson, "What 'Freedom come-all-ye" says to us today', *Caledonian Mercury*, 9 April 2012, <http://caledonianmercury.com/2012/04/09/opinion-what-freedom-come-all-ye-says-to-us-today/0031919>.

This could bring nothing but good to all the people living in these islands and create a better and stronger basis for us to continue to work together as good reliable neighbours.[50]

'What of Hamish's lasting political influence?' asked Bill Scott:

Would we have a Scottish Parliament today without his efforts to revive Scottish folk culture? Well Angus Calder considered that and concluded, '... that without the regeneration of national consciousness marked by the folksong revival, the relaunch of the SNP as a serious political force in the 1960s would not have happened, and neither would Labour's lagging re-conversion to home rule'.

But Henderson's optimistic vision of the future is still to be realised. Scottish recruits still make up nearly one third of Britain's frontline troops in Afghanistan. Weapons of mass destruction are still here (and not in Iraq). So when will this Scotland of our dreams come into being? Only when Henderson and MacLean's vision of an independent, socialist Scotland comes into full bloom.[51]

Indeed, many quotations can be summoned in support of that assumption. When Hamish Henderson still hoped the 'lamentable breach' in the SLP could be healed, he spoke, in 1976, of 'Scotland moving forward towards independence.'[52] A year later, in his letter to the 'Muckle Toun' of Langholm urging it to honour Hugh MacDiarmid – 'all too long without honour in his own home town' – he spoke of his expectation that 1977 would be 'undoubtedly the year that Scotland will make a major step forward towards independence – the goal that Christopher Murray Grieve has devoted his life to help bring about.'[53]

Yet, he was not always that clear. Often, his preferred term was Home Rule – something perhaps more akin to 'Devo Max'. But the terms get frequently blurred as, for example, when he demanded at a CND rally in 1962: 'Scotland must be in the United Nations.

---

[50] *Ibid.*

[51] Bill Scott, 'Hamish Henderson's Torch of Freedom'.

[52] Hamish Henderson, *The Armstrong Nose*, p.228.

[53] *Ibid.*, p.230.

(...) We need a Scottish Voice. We need Home Rule!'[54] Now, Home Rule, according to usual parlance, would denote a high degree of autonomy, but not independence. And anything short of independence would not give Scotland a seat in the United Nations.

Often he spoke of 'autonomy' – as in 1968, when he expected that the response to the 'Wilsonite fiasco' would be an SNP victory in Scotland:

> As soon as it gets a chance, the electorate will undoubtedly bid a 'soldier's farewell' to the raddled rump of the Labour Party in Scotland, and entrust the SNP with the job of negotiating our necessary and long-overdue autonomy.[55]

In 1983, the phrase was slightly changed to Scotland 'taking its place as a self-respecting – and respected – nation, with a reasonable chance of managing its own affairs.'[56]

And is 'The Freedom Come-All-Ye' only about nuclear weapons in Scotland, is the 'roch wind' only blowing here – or rather 'in the great glen o the warld the day'?[57] And if it were so directly and solely about Scotland's independence, why did Henderson himself describe it as an 'anti-nationalist song'?[58] David Stenhouse called it 'Scotland's Internationale' – an internationalist, rather than a nationalist anthem.

Nationalism – Internationalism

Why this ambiguity? Henderson was a nationalist. But he was also a committed socialist and internationalist. A key to this internationalist nationalism of Henderson's is his British Army background – not just a window on British imperialism, but the very experience of British solidarity in fighting the dark forces of fascism. Also, there was his proximity to the Communist Party of

---

[54] *ibid.*, p.101.

[55] *Ibid.*, p.172.

[56] *Ibid.*, p.240.

[57] Hamish Henderson, *Collected Poems and Songs*, p.143.

[58] David Stenhouse, 'Scotland's Internationale', *Sunday Herald*, 7 November 1999.

Britain – whose aspirations were British and international – and
thus arch-unionist.

He was close to Lawrence Daly's Fife Socialist League. Daly had
written in 1962:

> A Scottish Parliament could certainly contain a majority of
> Labour and radical members. There is every chance that it
> could not only revitalise Scotland's economic and cultural
> life but that it might well set the pace for the progressive
> social transformation of the rest of Britain.[59]

This British dimension is also present in Hamish's friend Norman
Buchan's famous quote from *Whither Scotland*, a decade later:

> The key argument is that if we remove all Scottish political
> control and influence over what all accept is a single
> economic entity in the United Kingdom, then we are
> left inevitably to be controlled by that total economy.
> Consequently, we would have less say than we have now
> over our own fate. Paradoxically, total separatism means
> less independence.[60]

But the main reason for Henderson's ambiguity about nationalism
is his championing of linguistic and cultural diversity as the 'best
guarantee against ... overbearing nationalist sentiments.'[61] Alec
Finlay observed, 'as cultural confidence has grown it has become
more possible, necessary even, to acknowledge Scotland's
linguistic and cultural diversity, and champion this as strength
rather than weakness.'[62] There was also, in the background, his
awareness that 'the anonymous ballad-makers ... were operating

---

[59] Quoted in Christopher Harvie, *Scotland and Nationalism: Scottish Society
and Politics 1707 to the Present*, London: Routledge, (fourth ed.) 2004,
p.158.

[60] Norman Buchan, 'Politics I', in Duncan Glen (ed.), *Whither Scotland? A
prejudiced look at the future of Scotland*, London, Victor Gollancz, 1971, p.
90.

[61] Alec Finlay, 'Afterword', *The Armstrong Nose*, p.334.

[62] *Ibid.*

in a zone which ignored national and political boundaries;'[63] and there was, most important of all, 'his identification with that most dispossessed group of all, the travellers, who cannot be placed within conventional national borders.'[64]

This 'heterogeneous sense of nationalism' he found shared in Federico Garcia Lorca, whom he quoted approvingly in a letter to the *Scotsman* in 1966:

> I am a Spaniard through and through, and it would be impossible for me to live outside my own geographical frontiers: but I hate the Spaniard who is that and nothing else, and wants to be nothing else. I am the brother of all men, and I abhor the man who sacrifices himself for an abstract nationalistic idea, just because of a blindfolded love of his country. The good Chinese is nearer to me than the bad Spaniard. I sing Spain, and I feel it in my very marrow; but I am, above all, a citizen of the world, and a brother of all men. Therefore I do not believe in frontiers.[65]

Over and over, Hamish Henderson attacked those with too narrow a focus on 'Scottishness', citing instead Antonio Gramsci, Bert Brecht, Karl Kraus and the Basque Miguel de Unamuno who were at times scathingly critical of their own countries, and yet 'not the betrayers but the fulfillers of their respective national traditions.'[66] He rejected 'McDiarmid's separatism and anglophobia'.[67]

> A melancholy nursing of ancient grievances may have accompanied some folkish expressions of anti-imperialism, yet Henderson's stance on the national question was not

---

[63] Hamish Henderson, 'At the Foot o' yon Excellin' Brae', *Alias MacAlias*, p.53.

[64] Alec Finlay, 'Afterword', p.339.

[65] Quoted in Hamish Henderson, *The Armstrong Nose*, p.151; the passage is from *El Sol* in Madrid, published on the eve of the Spanish Civil War, on 19 June 1936.

[66] *Ibid.*, p.240.

[67] Alec Finlay, 'Afterword', p.334.

that of a kilted chauvinist standing at the bar and reciting 'fee fi fo fum' at witless English invaders.[68]

Rejecting 'the excesses of nationalism' was part of 'his endeavor to encourage a vision of national consciousness composed in terms of a diverse people rather than a homogeneous nation.'[69] In 'To Hugh MacDiarmid', Henderson confronts head-on his fellow poet's 'separatism and anglophobia': 'I don' wanna step behin' dat tartan curtain...'[70]

Hamish Henderson never joined the SNP. As to the reasons for that, Jack Brand may have a clue to offer in his study on Scottish nationalism:

> Whereas the early days of the SNP had seen literary figures like R. B. Cunninghame Graham and Compton Mackenzie in important positions, the small, defensive post-war SNP was in no sense an attractive environment for them. It seemed to outsiders like a tiny body of purists intent on navel gazing.[71]

According to Tim Neat, Hamish was 'briefly tempted to join the party' after Winnie Ewing's Hamilton by-election victory of 1967.[72] But then the '1320 Club' appeared on the scene, with Hugh MaDiarmid as a prominent member – an organisation which Henderson saw as the 'self-elected Elect' and a threat to the democratic nationalist cause:

> I ... am absolutely convinced that about the only thing that can now seriously hinder Scotland's development into a self-respecting adult community in effective control of its own affairs is the big-headed presumption of the 'self-

---

[68] Patrick Wright, 'His Bonnet Akimbo', *London Review of Books*, 3 November 2011.

[69] *Ibid.*, p.338.

[70] Hamish Henderson, *Collected Poems and Songs*, p.120.

[71] Jack Brand, *The National Movement in Scotland*, London: Routledge & Kegan Paul, 1978, p.104.

[72] Timothy Neat, *Hamish Henderson*, Vol.II, p.112.

elected Elect'. It is surely more than ever vital that the advance to Home Rule, so urgently needed, should not only be democratic but be seen to be democratic.[73]

He commended the SNP on its good sense to put some distance between the party and this elitist, semi-secretive group.

But Hamish Henderson seems not to have been, to use a phrase of Robin Harper's, as 'gung-ho' about independence[74] as some of his ardent fans would like to believe. Or, maybe Hamish was ahead of his time, realising that Devolution, Home Rule and Independence were all part of a continuum of autonomy, and that in the interdependent late twentieth- or twenty-first centuries absolute independence was, even more than in previous eras, impossible. Or what are we to make of the SNP's independence plans – keep the Queen, keep the pound, and keep Nato?

Democratic Intellect

So, let us go back to the question – would Hamish Henderson be out and about if he were still alive and campaign for a Yes vote in the Referendum? Let us indulge in some speculation – here is a scenario:

He would have, probably very publicly, torn up his Labour membership card when Tony Blair dragged Britain into the Iraq war in 2003; he would have joined the mass demonstrations, particularly the anti-war protest on 15 February of that year, which counted nearly 100,000 participants in Glasgow. Certainly, he would have been part of the Make Poverty History campaign in 2005. He would have welcomed the SNP victories of 2007 and 2011. He would have shared a dram with the Occupy movement in St Andrew's Square. And in 2012 he would have been one of the prominent figureheads of the Scotland Yes platform.

Or would he? Could he have tried to rally support for the Devo Max option – sensing, as a pragmatist, that a majority for further devolution was much more likely than one for outright independence? Or perhaps because Raymond Ross was right in

---

[73] Hamish Henderson, *The Armstrong Nose*, p.164.

[74] Eddie Barnes, 'Greens give backing to YesScotland corner', *Scotland on Sunday*, 7 October 2012.

characterising him as 'an Old Labour man and a veteran Home Ruler'?[75]

Was that perhaps the reason he did join the Labour party in 1997? Why not the SNP? Or Tommy Sheridan's Scottish Socialist Party (like Angus Calder)? Did he feel that, under Donald Dewar, Labour had returned to the ideals of the 'early Labour pioneers'[76] and Home Rulers John Maclean and Keir Hardie? Or did he think, back then, that the Labour party's proposals were the best offer possible at the time? Anyway, he seems to have seen no contradiction between his membership in the Scottish Labour Party and his life-long commitment to Home Rule and, as many of his interventions hint at, to Scottish independence – or, as Jack Brand had it, 'some form of independence for Scotland.'[77]

One thing is clear: Hamish Henderson's life was that of an activist. Professional, cultural and political activities are inseparably entwined in his life – from his earliest days as a young Communist and anti-fascist through the campaigns for land reform, for peace and nuclear disarmament, against apartheid, for gay rights, against Thatcherism and the Poll Tax, and for Scottish self-government. 'Yet,' as Alex Wood contends, 'his political contributions were ultimately secondary to his cultural contributions.'[78] For Raymond Ross,

> Henderson was humanitarian in everything he did, and said, and always held the field for the 'democratic intellect'. He saw no other way, and his life's work, his very motivation, could perhaps be best described by that telling phrase of George Elder Davie's.[79]

In the Scottish Parliament, Michael Russell also stressed the cultural and humanitarian side of Hamish:

---

[75] Raymond Ross, 'Hamish Henderson'.

[76] *Hamish Hemderson, The Armstrong Nose*, p.93.

[77] Jack Brand, *The National Movement in Scotland*, p.115.

[78] Alex Wood, 'Scotland's folk hero: Hamish Henderson', *Scottish Review*, 7 January 2010.

[79] Raymond Ross, 'Hamish Henderson: Folklorist, Poet and Songwriter', *The Scotsman*, 11 March 2002.

Like all cultural nationalists – in the best sense of the term – Hamish Henderson was also an internationalist. The two stances are indivisible. They both arise from a curiosity about and identification with the question of our humanity and our relationships with one another.[80]

We can be pretty certain that Hamish Henderson would have welcomed the Referendum – the freedom for all Scots to decide their constitutional future. And whichever way the Sots vote in 2014, they will exercise their right of self-determination. Hamish would, I suppose, have been 'at hame' with that freedom, whatever the outcome.

As Arnold Rattenbury commented, 'Around such a figure myth and legend quite naturally swirled and, sometimes with his own help, stuck.'[81] Once it is fully catalogued and accessible, the Hamish Henderson Archive will surely offer further clues about Hamish's politics.

---

[80] Michael Russell, Scottish Parliament debate, 27 March 2002, <http://archive.scottish.parliament.uk/business/businessBulletin/bb-02/bb-03-12f.htm>.

[81] Arnold Rattenbury, 'Flytings', London Review of Books, 23 January 2003.

Contributors

Jim Bainbridge is a Tyneside-born singer and Melodeon player who came to fame as the leader of the Marsden Rattlers, one of the first dance bands to come out of the folk revival. He won the melodeon competitions at Blairgowrie and Kinross and is a regular visitor to folk clubs and traditional festivals like Auchtermuchty and Kirriemuir. Living in Glentrool in southwest Scotland, he has also become a regular reviewer and writer for *Living Tradition* magazine.

Eberhard 'Paddy' Bort is the Academic Coordinator of the Institute of Governance at the University of Edinburgh. He is also Chair of Edinburgh Folk Club and the editor of two previous volumes related to the life and work of Hamish Henderson – *Borne on the Carrying Stream: The Legacy of Hamish Henderson* (Grace Note Publications, 2010) and *'Tis Sixty Years Since: The 1951 Edinburgh People's Festival Ceilidh and the Scottish Folk Revival* (Grace Note Publications, 2011).

Owen Dudley Edwards is an Honorary Fellow in the School of History at the University of Edinburgh. Owen is a contributor to all major historical journals. In keeping with that University's treasured tradition of 'generalism', he is very much a polymath. Dudley Edwards' natural brio and mastery of words confer on his most scholarly contributions a spirit of entertainment. He was born in Dublin and educated at Belvedere College and UCD. He has been acknowledged as 'a distinguished Irish scholar and man of letters, whose pan-Celtic spirit comprehends a Welsh name, a university post in Scotland and several important books on Irish history.' He is a regular contributor and reviewer for radio, television and the press. His books include *The Quest for Sherlock Holmes: A Biographical Study of Arthur Conan Doyle, Mind of an Activist: James Connolly, P.G Wodehouse: A Critical and Historical Study,* Macaulay, *Burke and Hare* and *British Children's Fiction in the Second World War.*

Fred Freeman is a Fellow in English at the University of Edinburgh, has extensive experience of teaching literature, folk music and history. He wrote his PhD thesis on Robert Fergusson, Robert Burns's 'elder in the muse'. Shortly after Hamish Henderson's death, Fred produced *A' the Bairns o' Adam* for Greentrax, a highly regarded CD of Hamish Henderson songs, recorded by many artists who were personal friends of Hamish, or greatly admired his work. He also produced, between 1996 and 2003, *The Complete Songs of Robert* Burns, a seminal 13 CD box set, for Linn Records.

George Gunn was born in Thurso in 1956 where he still lives. He has been a deep-sea fisherman, a driller for oil in the North Sea and a journalist – he contributes to the local and national press, the Scottish Review, and sends a fortnightly column, 'From The Pictish Navy', to the *John O Groat Journal*. He is well known as a playwright, with some twenty professional productions to date. From 1992 to 2010 he was Artistic Director of Grey Coast Theatre Company, which he co-founded; he also tutors in drama at North Highland College. He has published a number of pamphlets and collections, including *Black Fish* (Scotia Review, 2004), *Winter Barley* (Chapman, 2005) and *The Atlantic Forest* (Two Ravens Press, 2008).

Tom Hubbard was the first librarian of the Scottish Poetry Library and is the author, editor or co-editor of over thirty academic and literary works. His own and translated poetry has appeared in journals like *Akros*, *Chapman* and *Lines* Review. He published his first novel, *Marie B.* (Ravenscraig Press) in 2008. His collection *The Chagall Winnocks: Wi Ither Scots Poems and Ballants o Europe* (Grace Note Publications) was published in 2011. He lives in Kirkcaldy.

Alison McMorland is a collector, performer, teacher, editor and publisher. Songs and singing have been and remain at the heart of what she is about. In the words of the late Hamish Henderson, she "stands out as one of the principal modern interpreters of an ancestral ballad singing tradition, breathing new life into ancient memorials by uniting scrupulous traditional fidelity with versatile and resourceful creative artistry." She now lives in Perthshire with her husband Geordie McIntyre. Their latest record is *Where Ravens Reel* (Rowan Records). Alison has published a book on Willie Scott,

Herd Laddie o the Glen: Songs of a Border Shepherd (1988; new revised edition 2007) and edited a book on Elizabeth Stewart, *Up Yon Wide and Lonely Glen: Travellers' Songs, Stories and Tunes of the Fetterangus Stewarts* (University Press of Mississippi/Elphinstone Institute, University of Aberdeen, 2012).

Ewan McVicar is a renowned storyteller and songwriter. He has performed in over 200 schools and in castles, museums, folk festivals and other venues across Britain, as well as in Canada, the USA, Holland and Russia. He has written some 40 songs which have been commercially recorded, including 20 for the Singing Kettle children's show. He lives in Linlithgow.

Pino Mereu is an Italian scholar, translator and folklorist, born in Sardinia. He also organises the Hamish Henderson Folk Club in Rome. He gave the Hamish Henderson Memorial Lecture in 2008 (published in *Borne on the Carrying Stream*, 2010) and published *Lamento per Antonio Gramsci* in 2010 and *Anzio Pipe Band* in 2012.

Hayden Murphy is a poet, journalist and critic. Born in Dublin in 1945, he has been an Arts Journalist for over forty years in Ireland and Scotland. Widely published and anthologised as a poet, his latest publication is *Linked Lines* (Rocadora Press, 2011). He lives in Edinburgh with his wife for over twenty years, Frances Corcoran.

Belle Stewart (1906-1997) first came to the attention of folklorists in the mid-1960s when Hamish Henderson was looking for someone who could sing 'The Berryfields o Blair', and Maurice Fleming directed him in her direction. Not only did she know the song, she had actually written it, and she possessed a huge repertoire of traditional folksongs and ballads, as well as originals she had written for weddings and other occasions. In 2006, her daughter Sheila Stewart wrote her biography, *Queen Amang the Heather: The Life of Belle Stewart* (Birlinn).

2628054R00123

Printed in Great Britain
by Amazon.co.uk, Ltd.,
Marston Gate.